Study Guide
for

Curran and Renzetti

SOCIAL PROBLEMS
SOCIETY IN CRISIS
FOURTH EDITION

Raquel Kennedy Bergen
St. Joseph's University

Allyn and Bacon
Boston · London · Toronto · Sydney · Tokyo · Singapore

A Simon & Schuster Company
Needham Heights, Massachusetts 02194

ISBN 0-205-17889-8

Printed in the United States of America

10 9 8 7 6 5 4 3 2 1   99 98 97 96 95

TABLE OF CONTENTS

INTRODUCTION

TO THE STUDENT:

This study guide has been prepared to help you understand more completely the material presented in Social Problems: Society in Crisis by Curran and Renzetti, and to build your confidence in your knowledge of the text. Each chapter is organized in the following format:

- Chapter Overview
- Detailed Chapter Outline
- Self-tests:
  - True/False questions
  - Multiple Choice questions
  - Fill in the Blank questions
  - Matching questions
- Answer key for each question

In order to perform to the best of your ability on examinations of the material, I suggest that you follow the steps outlined below.

First, quickly read the chapter overview and the detailed outline, to familiarize yourself with the material.

Secondly, read the chapter closely--pay close attention to the highlighted words in the text.

Thirdly, take the self-test without looking back at the text and write your answers on a separate piece of paper. While taking the test, keep in mind the time constraints that you will face in an actual classroom and try to allot time accordingly.

Fourthly, check your answers against the key at the end of the chapter. Think carefully about the correct answer and go over each of the alternatives and try to reason why they are not correct.

Finally, go back to the text and re-read each section pertaining to the questions you missed. In doing this, you will reinforce the correct concepts in your mind and better prepare yourself for examinations.

Reading the material closely and using this study guide will help you to master the most important material in the text. In doing so, I believe you will gain a new understanding of social problems in society, and have a satisfying learning experience.

Raquel Kennedy Bergen, PhD
April 1995

CHAPTER 1

This introductory chapter begins by describing what constitutes a social problem and providing sociological perspectives on social problems. Included in this is both a discussion of the European origins of Sociology as well as a focus on the history of Sociology in the United States. Particular attention is given to the three main theoretical perspectives used to study social problems; structural functionalism, the conflict perspective, and symbolic interactionism. The chapter concludes with a discussion of the various methods which Sociologists use in conducting social research including surveys, field observation, and content analysis; and a discussion of the ethical principles which govern sociological research.

A. STUDYING SOCIAL PROBLEMS

In order to study Social Problems, one must first determine when a problem becomes a "social problem". Defining "social problems" has been problematic because traditionally these definitions have hinged on "majority" opinion. This raises some unanswerable questions, such as how many people constitute a majority and do opinions of all members of society carry equal weight?

B. SOCIOLOGICAL PERSPECTIVES ON SOCIAL PROBLEMS

Sociology is defined as the scientific study of human societies. Particularly, sociologists are interested in studying social groups and collective behavior. Rather than looking at social problems as the result of an individual's maladjustment, sociologists place social problems in the larger social context of collective behavior and social structures. This section provides a foundation for studying social problems by exploring the origins of sociology.

1. Sociology developed as a discipline in response to the social problems which plagued 19th century Europe. The theories and contributions of Auguste Comte, Emile Durkheim, Karl Marx, and Max Weber are explored.

2. At the turn of the century American Sociology was focused on the problems associated with the urban environment. The first department of Sociology in the U.S. was located at the University of Chicago. The Chicago School focused on social disorganization as the root of social problems. Contributions and criticisms of the Chicago School are explored.

3. Other important sociological work including that done by W.E.B. DuBois, Talcott Parsons and social revisionists have also shaped current sociology. There are three theoretical perspectives used by sociologists to study social problems.

    1. Functionalism emerged in the 1940s in a conservative climate with an emphasis on "a return to normalcy." Talcott Parsons and Robert Merton were the leading proponents of this perspective. Functionalists focused on society as composed of interrelated institutions and believed that human behavior was governed by normative

consensus. This paradigm left many questions unanswered. As questions of oppression, exploitation, and exclusion became more prominent in the 1960's, a new paradigm emerged to attempt to address these questions.

2. The founder of the conflict perspective is Karl Marx. Contemporary thinkers such as C. Wright Mills emphasize the role of power and inequality in society. This view holds that the inequalities present in the social structure are maintained by a social hierarchy. This inequality benefits a powerful few in society and disadvantages many others. This inequality generates social conflict. According to the conflict perspective, sociology cannot be value free. It is necessary and appropriate for sociologists to be social critics.

3. Symbolic interactionism focuses on daily communications and gestures which people use to interact with each other. Symbolic interactionists begin with the premise that social reality is the product of social interactions. Symbolic interactionists are particularly concerned with socialization and how members of society learn the norms and values of a society. They focus on resocialization to solve social problems. Symbolic interactionists have been criticized for over-emphasizing socialization and downplaying larger social structures.

C. METHODS OF SOCIOLOGICAL RESEARCH

This section details the most popular methods of conducting social research and the advantages and disadvantages of each.

1. Survey research involves asking questions of a sample of the population either through interviews or by questionnaires. This is the most popular method used by Sociologists.
2. Field observation involves the researcher actually watching the behavior he/she is interested in studying. Participant and nonparticipant observation are two types of field observation.
3. Content analysis involves the analysis of some form of communication such as historical documents, newspaper, and photographs to understand social phenomena.
4. Feminist sociologists have reformulated traditional research processes and called for greater equity in the research process, encouraging self-disclosure, and empowering the oppressed through their research.
5. Many ethical dilemmas plague sociological research including harming and deceiving participants. The central ethical principles used to guide sociological research are explored.

F. THE PERSPECTIVE OF THIS TEXT

In this final section, the authors discuss the influences of conflict theory, feminist sociology, and symbolic interactionism on their work. One of the their goals in writing this book is to emphasize social change through collective action.

SELF-TEST

True/False

1. Until the 1940s, U.S. social scientists looked to Chicago as the center of sociological research.

   a. true
   b. false

2. Traditionally, most sociologists have defined social problems as being determined by majority opinion.

   a. true
   b. false

3. One's social position in society influences one's definition of what constitutes a social problem.

   a. true
   b. false

4. Max Weber focused on two main classes--the bourgeoisie and the proletariat.

   a. true
   b. false

5. One of the central ethical principles of Sociological research is that the research should not harm the research participants.

   a. true
   b. false

6. The Chicago School is also known as the Ecological School.

   a. true
   b. false

7. Functionalist theory has found no value in prostitution.

   a. true
   b. false

8. The dominant paradigm of the 1960s was the structural functionalist theory.

   a. true
   b. false

9. Conflict theory emphasizes the role of power in understanding social problems.

a. true
b. false

10. Content analysis is the most frequently used technique for data collection by sociologists.

a. true
b. false

11. Feminists believe that a value-free sociology is both possible and desirable.

a. true
b. false

12. Symbolic Interactionists focus on daily communication, symbols, and patterns of socialization.

a. true
b. false

13. Inflexibility improves survey research.

a. true
b. false

14. Concealing one's identity when doing survey research is always considered unethical.

a. true
b. false

15. Content analysis is rarely used by Sociologists in conducting historical research.

a. true
b. false

16. The authors of the text do not believe in sociological determinism.

a. true
b. false

17. The earliest sociologists were likely to be male, from rural communities, and interested in social reform.

a. true
b. false

18. All sociologists work within the same paradigm.

a. true
b. false

19. Sociological concepts and theories are both subjectively and objectively developed.

a. true
b. false

20. Sociologists do not draw a distinction between facts and values in their own research.

a. true
b. false

21. Sociology became a prestigious profession after World War II.

a. true
b. false

22. Structural functionalists advocate social reform in their work.

a. true
b. false

23. Functionalists believe that a "normative consensus" exists in society.

a. true
b. false

24. Functionalists argue that slow and gradual change results in social problems.

a. true
b. false

25. Conflict theorists begin with the observation that the U.S. society is characterized by equality.

a. true
b. false

26. Conflict theorists believe that conflict is not necessarily bad for society.

a. true
b. false

27. A functionalist would argue that "separating the research process from the possible ways that the research may be used is irresponsible."

a. true
b. false

28. When one becomes actively involved in what he or she is studying, he or she is working as a participant observer.

a. true
b. false

29. A common problem facing researchers who do content analysis is possible biases in the data sources.

a. true
b. false

30. Feminists have advocated that researchers allow those whom they are studying to "talk back" to them.

a. true
b. false

31. Under some circumstances it is acceptable for a researcher to coerce individuals to participate in a study.

a. true
b. false

32. Symbolic interactionism is criticized for focusing too much on social institutions and larger social structures.

a. true
b. false

33. The work of Sociologists are strongly governed by professional codes of ethics established by the American Sociological Association.

a. true
b. false

34. A psychological reductionist would argue "society made me do it."

a. true
b. false

35. The authors of this text maintain that people are born into a particular place in society, but that humans are active agents who can transform their environment.

a. true
b. false

36. Functionalists believe that the role of sociologists should be as morally-detached scientific observers.

a. true
b. false

37. Karl Mannheim coined the phrase "symbolic interactionism."

a. true
b. false

38. Some have argued that the 1980's were characterized by "a new brand of social pessimism."

a. true
b. false

39. The authors of your text are most likely structural functionalists.

a. true
b. false

40. The authors of the text argue that the United States should be the main focus of the study of social problems because 50% of the world's "important" population resides in the U.S.

a. true
b. false

Multiple Choice

1. Sociologists attempt to deal with uneasiness about world affairs by:

   a. Studying and explaining social problems and their causes
   b. Turning away from and ignoring them
   c. Donating large sums of money to social causes
   d. Improving communication systems

2. Sociology emerged in response to the social problems of _____ century Europe.

   a. 16th
   b. 17th
   c. 18th
   d. 19th

3. The founder of sociology was:

   a. Karl Marx
   b. Herbert Spencer
   c. Auguste Comte
   d. C. Wright Mills

4. Auguste Comte saw sociologists as:

   a. undisciplined scientists
   b. a "priesthood of humanity"
   c. subjective analysts of society
   d. the subordinates of politicians

5. The first department of sociology was established at ________in 1892.

   a. University of Pennsylvania
   b. University of Delaware
   c. University of Chicago
   d. Harvard University

6. Which of the following was not a member of the Chicago School?

   a. Robert Park
   b. Ernest Burgess
   c. Talcott Parsons
   d. Louis Wirth

7. Historically, sociologists have defined a social problem as one:

a. which concerns the majority of society's members
b. which is deemed so by politicians, teachers and sociologists
c. which is considered harmful by a critical mass of people
d. none of the above

8. In the summer of 1994, the United States became concerned with the problem of

a. Air Pollution
b. International Terrorism
c. Wife Abuse
d. Animal Abuse
e. None of the above

9. ______________ argued that in identifying social issues, one must distinguish public issues from personal troubles.

a. Karl Marx
b. Talcott Parsons
c. C. Wright Mills
d. Max Weber

10. One's definition of a situation as problematic is influenced by one's

a. race
b. class
c. gender
d. sexual orientation
e. all of the above

11. Subjectivity in sociology:

a. is not acknowledged as an issue
b. links the researcher with what he or she is investigating
c. places the discipline into a non-scientific realm
d. makes sociological knowledge relative

12. If one talks about society as if it is separate from the people who make it up and thus produces the illusion that we have no control over society; one is engaging in

a. structural hierarchy
b. structural determinism
c. ecological determinism
d. econological fallacy
e. all of the above

13. The primary focus of the Chicago School was:

a. racism
b. social deviance
c. social-psychology
d. the sociology of knowledge

14. A major criticism of the Chicago School was:

a. it tried to shape different groups into white middle-class Protestants
b. it was too theoretical and esoteric
c. it was politically corrupt, thus invalidating any research findings
d. it was too distant from actual social work

15. The theory of concentric zones

a. indicates that all urban areas are equally plagued by deviance
b. indicates that inner cities are relatively free from social disorganization
c. indicates that social disorganization leads to social problems
d. proves that those zones closest to industry and business are most crime-free

16. W.E.B. DuBois

a. was a central member of the Chicago School
b. was the founder of Symbolic Interactionism
c. was the founder of the National Association for the Advancement of Colored People (NAACP)
d. was the founder of the Sociology Department at Harvard

17. After World War II, the focus of sociological research:

a. shifted the role of sociologist from social reformer to objective social scientist
b. was lessened due to a lack of governmental interest
c. placed a heavy emphasis on social action
d. made sociology a less respected field

18. The functionalist perspective was popular during the post-war period because:

a. the conservative climate was obsessed with a "return to normalcy"
b. the real communist threat made sociologists react in favor of political activism
c. widespread poverty necessitated an extremist position
d. there was a general perception that the U.S. was in decline

19. Functionalists believe all of the following <u>except</u>:

a. society is made up of interrelated institutions
b. the members of society share a set of agreed upon values and customs
c. society exists in a state of equilibrium
d. all of the above are believed by functionalists

20. Which of the following sociologists was <u>not</u> a structural functionalist?

a. Talcott Parsons
b. Robert Merton
c. C. Wright Mills
d. Kingsley Davis

21. Functionalists believe that social problems:

a. are the result of slow and gradual change
b. result when society is in a constant state of equilibrium
c. are never functional for society
d. are caused when individuals do not internalize the normative consensus

22. Kingsley Davis argued that prostitution was functional because:

a. women will always be socially dominated by men with more resources
b. everyone is born with a need for sexual gratification and prostitution provides a convenient outlet
c. prostitution provides job opportunities for "inferior" women
d. all of the above

23. Which of the following factors was <u>not</u> relevant to the development of the conflict perspective?

a. Women's Liberation Movement
b. Civil Rights Movement
c. the growth of the middle-class
d. all of the above

24. A conflict theorist believes:

a. that the sociologist should act as a social critic
b. that completely objective sociological research is possible
c. that biased sociological research is best
d. that a goal of social problems research is not to suggest possible solutions

25. Conflict theorists derive many of their basic ideas from the classical work of:

a. Talcott Parsons
b. Auguste Comte
c. Karl Marx
d. Howard Becker

26. Which of the following contemporary theorists is credited with being one of the founders of the conflict perspective?

a. C. Wright Mills
b. Howard Becker
c. Kingsley Davis
d. Thomas Kuhn

27. ________________ coined the phrase symbolic interactionism.

a. C. Wright Mills
b. Talcott Parsons
c. Louis Wirth
d. Herbert Blumer

28. Symbolic interactionists have been criticized for

a. being too focused on macro-theories
b. not suggesting solutions to social problems
c. placing too much emphasis on resocialization
d. ignoring the unequal distribution of power in society
e. both c and d

29. A _____________ theorist would be most likely to study gender and race oppression.

a. conflict
b. functionalist
c. psychological
d. symbolic interactionist

30. A _______________ theorist would be most likely to study gestures and symbols.

a. conflict
b. functionalist
c. psychological
d. symbolic interactionist

31. ___________ research is the most frequently used method of data collection by sociologists.

a. field observation
b. experiment
c. survey
d. content analysis

32. Which of the following is a disadvantage of using questionnaires for data collection?

a. they are relatively expensive
b. the data is not standardized
c. they do not usually allow for respondent elaboration
d. they inhibit artificiality

33. Which of the following is <u>not</u> a form of observational research?

a. participant observation
b. non-participant observation
c. phenomenon observation
d. all of the above

34. Entering the natural setting to understand behavior and social interaction is done through:

a. surveys
b. experiments
c. field observation
d. content analysis

35. Sociologists conducting historical research commonly examine which documents?

a. newspapers
b. diaries
c. photographs
d. all of the above

36. Ethical issues about concealing one's true identity from those being researched, are most likely to arise while doing:

a. experimental research
b. field observation
c. content analysis
d. surveys

37. Feminist Sociologists are particularly concerned with all of the following <u>except:</u>

a. developing reciprocal relationships with those whom they study
b. promoting biased research
c. learning from research participants
d. empowering the oppressed

38. An example of "psychological reductionism" is that the persistence of poverty can be explained by the fact that:

a. the poor have character defects
b. the poor are violence-prone
c. the poor lack impulse control
d. all of the above

39. Which of the following is <u>not</u> an ethical principle by which sociologists abide in doing research?

a. research participants must not be harmed
b. research participants must voluntarily agree to be participate
c. deception of research participants is always unethical
d. all of the above are principles which govern the research of sociologists

40. The authors of this text have been influenced by which perspective?

a. functionalist
b. conflict
c. symbolic interactionist
d. feminist
e. all of the above except a
d. structural determinist perspective

Fill in the Blanks

1. ________________ is the study of human societies.

2. The two founding fathers of the conflict perspective are _______ and ______________________.

3. ____________________ established sociology as an independent scientific discipline and coined the phrase collective conscience.

4. The tendency to reduce social problems to the level of individual psychological maladjustment is known as _______________________.

5. Sociologists are involved in conducting ______________ research. That is, research which is based on direct observation of some kind.

Matching

1. Auguste Comte
2. Jerome Manis
3. Karl Mannheim
4. Chicago School
5. Talcott Parsons
6. Kingsley Davis
7. C. Wright Mills
8. Karl Marx
9. symbolic interactionism
10. Herbert Blumer
11. survey
12. content analysis
13. structural determinism
14. Emile Durkheim
15. Max Weber
16. functionalist
17. conflict
18. psychological reductionism
19. feminists
20. field research

A. Founder of Sociology
B. the perspective which focuses on gestures and symbols
C. A method which involves the use of questionnaires or interviews
D. coined the phrase symbolic interactionism
E. A method which analyzes the content of communication
F. A paradigm which focuses on power and inequality in society

G. To reduce social problems to the level of individual psychological maladjustments
H. Said "public opinion is shared and influenced by opinion makers"
I. Another way of saying "society made me do it"
J. A sociologist who would see society as being made up of a set of interrelated parts
K. Student of the sociology of knowledge
L. Said "Philosophers have only thought about the world in different ways, the point is to change it"
M. would advocate for consciousness-raising among those they study
N. Argued that there is a difference between public issues and personal troubles
O. He said "social facts have social causes"
P. coined the term "Verstehen"
Q. Leading proponent of structural functionalism
R. Believed that prostitution has social and natural causes
S. Also known as the Ecological School
T. A method which involves the observation of social phenomena in their natural setting

ANSWERS FOR CHAPTER 1

True/False

1.	True	21.	True
2.	False	22.	False
3.	True	23.	True
4.	False	24.	False
5.	True	25.	False
6.	True	26.	True
7.	True	27.	False
8.	False	28.	Tree
9.	True	29.	True
10.	False	30.	False
11.	False	31.	False
12.	True	32.	False
13.	False	33.	False
14.	False	34.	False
15.	False	35.	True
16.	True	36.	True
17.	True	37.	False
18.	False	38.	True
19.	True	39.	True
20.	False	40.	False

Multiple Choice

1.	a	21.	d
2.	d	22.	d
3.	c	23.	c
4.	b	24.	a
5.	c	25.	c
6.	c	26.	a
7.	c	27.	e
8.	c	28.	d
9.	c	29.	a
10.	c	30	e
11.	b	31.	c
12.	b	32.	c
13.	b	33.	c
14.	a	34.	c
15.	c	35.	d
16.	c	36.	d
17.	d	37.	b
18.	c	38.	d
19.	d	39.	c
20.	c	40.	e

Fill in the Blanks

1. Sociology
2. Karl Marx and C. Wright Mills
3. Emile Durkheim
4. Psychological Reductionism
5. Empirical

Matching

1.	A
2.	H
3.	K
4.	S
5.	Q
6.	R
7.	N
8.	L
9.	B
10.	D
11.	C
12.	E
13.	I
14.	O
15.	P

16. J
17. F
18. G
19. M
20. T

CHAPTER 2

This chapter discusses economic and political realities of contemporary society. The U.S. economy is discussed with particular emphasis placed on the current problems such as the trade deficit, unemployment and occupational health hazards. The political process is also addressed with particular attention paid to elections and the power of the judicial, legislative, and executive branches. Finally, the world community is analyzed with regard to military action and aid.

A. THE U.S ECONOMY: REALITIES AND THE CHALLENGES

This chapter opens with a discussion of the U.S. economy. This section gives a brief history of the U.S. economy and describes the structure of the industrial economy.

1. The U.S. economy can be characterized by a concentration of economic power among a few corporations. A monopoly occurs when economic power is concentrated in the hands of a group of corporations, who through their economic resources, are able to maintain this control. The factors which contribute to the continued domination of monopolies in the U.S. economy are addressed.
    a. Large firms are able to maintain their basic capital advantages which help to restrict competition.
    b. Competition is also restricted by the existence of interlocking directorates in which a leader of one corporation sits on the boards of other corporations to

enhance the flow of information and control.

c. Corporate merging, both vertical and horizontal, have also been important in decreasing economic competition in the U.S.

2. The United States economy has evolved over the years from a primary industry economy to a secondary industry economy and more recently, to a service economy. The service sector is divided into three categories; services for the affluent ("glamour professions"), welfare services, and services provided by the poor.

B. PROBLEMS IN THE U.S. ECONOMY

The current state of the U.S. economy is discussed.

1. While more people are working than ever in the U.S, there are a growing number of people living below the poverty line. Reasons for this are addressed.

a. The minimum wage does not provide a fair wage for workers and allow one to live above the poverty line.

b. Unemployment is defined as the percentage of working-age population out of work, and actively looking for a job. The limitations of this indicator are particularly addressed.

c. Underemployment, when one is forced to take a position below their training, education, or competence, is a growing problem in the U.S. particularly for college graduates.

2. The history of trade unions in the U.S. is briefly explored.

a. Unions initially organized to guarantee a basic level of wage and safety, however they ignored the more competitive sector and eventually developed a cooperative relationship with many large corporations.

b. The power of unions in the 1980s severely declined under the Reagan/Bush administrations. Problems facing unions today are addressed.

3. The federal government has been notoriously slow to act in imposing health and safety regulations in industry. Restrictions are often vaguely phrased and weakly enforced, thus, compounding the problem. The problems facing workers in the industrial, service, and agricultural sectors are addressed.

C. THE U.S. ECONOMY: BACK ON TOP? Following World War II, the U.S. enjoyed a position of unchallenged dominance in the world market. However, U.S. dominance was eroded in recent decades by foreign competition. In the 1990's there is some evidence that the U.S. has regained it's position of dominance. This section addresses the U.S. economy in the global marketplace.

1. In order to maximize profits and reduce costs many large corporations engage in the practice of <u>multinationalization</u>. Corporations achieve this by extending their markets throughout the world and using indigenous populations as a cheap source of labor. The dangers of these practices are discussed in detail.

2. The threat of foreign competition is discussed in light of recent world events.

3. The U.S. is currently experiencing a trade deficit. In other words, it imports more products than it exports. The consequences

of the trade deficit are discussed.

D. MAKING NATIONAL DECISIONS: THE POLITICAL PROCESS

The political process in the U.S. is complex and this section addresses how decisions are made and the meaning of "big government."

1. Since its inception, the federal government has been transformed from a decentralized system to a centralized body. The factors involved in this transformation are explored as are the implications of increasing federal bureaucracy.
    a. As the federal government continues to spend more than it receives through tax revenue, a federal deficit has occurred. In order to fund deficit spending, the government continues to borrow, resulting in a fiscal crisis.
2. The importance of voters and PAC's are considered with regard to electing public officials.
    a. Not all Americans exercise their right to vote. Who votes and the recent outcomes of the 1994 Congressional Elections are analyzed.
    b. Gender and race are important factors in not only who votes but who is elected. Recent advances of women and minorities are analyzed.
    c. PAC's (Political Action Committees) play an essential role in elections. The primary recipients of PAC money are incumbents.
3. The Legislative branch includes the Senate and the House of Representatives and is more democratic than the executive

branch. However, concerns about the role of political action committees (PAC's) in the election process and lobbyists in the legislative process are presented as problem areas.

4. The Judiciary branch, because of its unique power, has historically been the most important agent of social change in the U.S. However, the Supreme Court is not without its problems, and they are discussed here.

E. PROTECTING NATIONAL INTERESTS IN THE POST-COLD WAR PERIOD

The role of military in contemporary government and the frequent military involvements of the U.S. throughout its history are presented.

1. The emergence of modern technology has established the military as an independent and influential force on the U.S. political scene. Many argue that the military wields as much power over the decision-making process as does any one of the three constitutionally created branches of the federal government.
    a. The size and composition of the U.S. armed forces are discussed.
    b. The need for specialized equipment by the military insures that few companies are able to provide the equipment requested.
2. This interdependence of the military and defense contractors, known as the military-industrial complex, creates a powerful block which is used to maintain the present distribution of power. Implications of this relationship, including inefficiency and cost-

overrun, are explored. The issue of defense build-up is also addressed.

3. Three major intelligence agencies, the National Security Agency; National Reconnaissance Office; and the Central Intelligence Agency; are identified along with the activities and roles of each.

D. THE INTERNATIONAL POLITICAL SCENE

Recent changes in the former Soviet Union and Eastern Europe have profound implications for international political relationships.

1. Events during and following World Ward II were largely responsible for the polarization of the U.S. and the Soviet Union.
2. The escalation of conventional and nuclear arms, the arms race, is considered with regard to current global conditions.
3. The effects of recent political changes in the former Soviet Union and the Gulf War are discussed in terms of the arms race
4. Historically, associations among the more prominent nations with the U.S. or the Soviet Union tended to be formalized through treaties or recognized agreements. Affiliations have not always conformed to economic or political ideology. Realignments and new allegiances are considered in the wake of recent events.
5. Some of the political problems facing Eastern European and other Third World nations are addressed. One significant problem involves providing foreign aid to other countries.
   a. Often projects intended to improve the living conditions of the indigenous population have disastrous effects.

b. Ethical questions arise as to whether to continue to provide economic aid to governments engaged in activities which stand in direct opposition to the values of the U.S.

SELF-TEST

True/False

1. The time period between the Industrial Revolution and the 1930s is best characterized by a concentration of labor in the service sector.

   a. true
   b. false

2. In this text, monopoly means a group of large corporations that control a disproportionate amount of economic power.

   a. true
   b. false

3. The Sherman Anti-Trust Act tried to increase the power of individual corporations to dominate the market.

   a. true
   b. false

4. Oligopolistic control clearly exists in the U.S. economy.

   a. true
   b. false

5. Price fixing is legal in much of the world.

   a. true
   b. false

6. Service operations tend to be more labor-intensive than industrial operations.

   a. true
   b. false

7. The growth in the welfare service sector has most directly benefitted white males.

   a. true
   b. false

8. "Poverty service" jobs are known to be the best type of service jobs.

a. true
b. false

9. It is possible to work full time for the minimum wage and still live below the poverty line.

a. true
b. false

10. The official unemployment rate includes all working age people who are currently unemployed.

a. true
b. false

11. Only one-third of Americans who are unemployed receive unemployment benefits.

a. true
b. false

12. In 1993 approximately 63 million people were neither on a payroll nor looking for work.

a. true
b. false

13. The power and influence of U.S. unions has been steadily increasing since the 1950's

a. true
b. false

14. Compared to their European counterparts, U.S. unions have failed to loudly voice the concerns of their workers.

a. true
b. false

15. A sweatshop regularly violates wage, child labor, and safety and health regulations.

a. true
b. false

16. Between 1980 and 1990, approximately 12 million people died as a result of occupational accidents in the U.S.

a. true
b. false

17. Labor productivity in the U.S. lags far behind that of Japan and Germany.

a. true
b. false

18. The Chernobyl incident is an example of corporate dumping.

a. true
b. false

19. Japan is only one of five nations that currently enjoys a trade surplus with the U.S.

a. true
b. false

20. The U.S. has historically had a strong centralized federal government in place.

a. true
b. false

21. The federal budget has steadily grown to the current 1.5 trillion dollar mark.

a. true
b. false

22. Currently the federal government spends more than it receives in revenues.

a. true
b. false

23. The president of the U.S. is normally elected by about half of all eligible voters.

a. true
b. false

24. The "gender gap" in voting has been noted since 1952.

a. true
b. false

25. Currently, women and men hold approximately an equal number of state legislative seats.

a. true
b. false

26. Sociological research indicates that the amount of money spent on a campaign is not related to the success of the candidate.

a. true
b. false

27. It is the President's responsibility to nominate Supreme Court Justices.

a. true
b. false

28. The Supreme Curt only hears cases that it chooses to review.

a. true
b. false

29. The Supreme Court consists of nine Justices who are appointed for "life or good behavior."

a. true
b. false

30. Women and minorities are making significant inroads in terms of political office-holding.

a. true
b. false

31. The U.S. President has total autonomy in deploying U.S. troops abroad in emergency cases.

a. true
b. false

32. The present armed forces consist primarily of volunteers.

a. true
b. false

33. African American men and women are under-represented in the U.S. armed forces.

a. true
b. false

34. The defense industry is highly competitive and diverse.

a. true
b. false

35. Research indicates that military spending is not a positive factor in overall economic growth.

a. true
b. false

36. To date the CIA has never been involved covertly in the internal affairs of other nations.

a. true
b. false

37. The Korean War is seen as the start of the Cold War.

a. true
b. false

38. Currently, the major threat to world peace is the spread of traditional weapons and war technology.

a. true
b. false

39. The U.S. has a policy of giving aid to any country in need regardless of their domestic policies.

a. true
b. false

40. In the 1990's Eastern Europe has become a primary recipient of U.S. aid

a. true
b. false

Multiple Choice

1. When the labor force is concentrated in work which extracts products directly from the earth, this is known as:

   a. secondary industry
   b. tertiary industry
   c. cottage industry
   d. primary industry

2. The sector of the U.S. economy that currently employs a majority of workers is:

   a. the service sector
   b. manufacturing
   c. agriculture
   d. secondary industry

3. When a few large corporations control the market for a particular good, this is known as:

   a. a horizontal merger
   b. a closed market
   c. a vertical merger
   d. an oligopoly

4. Intercorporate control is dangerous because:

   a. it promotes price leading
   b. it promotes patterned pricing
   c. it increases the market control of already powerful corporations
   d. all of the above

5. Which of the following is <u>not</u> a factor which reinforces monopolies?

   a. interlocking directorates
   b. basic capital advantages
   c. corporate merging
   d. free enterprise

6. Which of the following is <u>not</u> true? Compared to industrial operations, service operations:

   a. are less likely to be unionized
   b. employ more people
   c. work less with machinery
   d. are more labor-intensive

7. Which of the following occupations is characterized as a member of the "glamour professions"?

   a. social worker
   b. educator
   c. food service employee
   d. commercial banker

8. The poor are most likely to work in which sector?

   a. glamour professions
   b. welfare services
   c. poverty services
   d. none of the above

9. To be included in the official unemployment rate, one must be all of the following <u>except:</u>

   a. out of work
   b. actively looking for a job
   c. at least 16 years old
   d. a discouraged worker

10. When workers accept jobs below their levels of training and skill they are:

    a. discouraged workers
    b. underemployed
    c. overemployed
    d. unemployed

11. Recent college graduates have:

    a. experienced the highest rates of employment since the 1920's
    b. are likely to go on for post-graduate education
    c. are experiencing a decline in entry-level positions
    d. both b and c above

12. Unions established themselves as the primary bargaining agent for workers in approximately

a. 1970
b. 1950
c. 1930
d. 1880

13. Unions in the U.S. have recently been criticized for

a. ignoring workers in small firms
b. ignoring issues of health and safety in the workplace
c. failing to increase the voice of workers
d. all of the above

14. Which of the following workers is likely to face occupational health risks?

a. factory
b. office
c. migrant
d. all of the above

15. The sale of goods overseas that have been banned from sale in the U.S. is known as

a. commodity transfer
b. dumping
c. protectionism
d. deficit spending

16. The practice of the government regulating imports is known as:

a. dumping
b. unionism
c. protectionism
d. tariffing

17. The best way to determine the rate of inflation is with:

a. the consumer price index
b. the Dow Jones industrial average
c. rates of union membership
d. national productivity rates

18. The total value of goods and services produced by the residents of a country in a given year, is the

a. economic index
b. gross national product
c. trade asset
d. consumer price index

19. Multinationalization has resulted in:

   a. positive relationships between all multinationals and their hosts
   b. boosting competition for a product in the host country
   c. the lives of citizens in the host country often being endangered
   d. increased regulation of Third World countries by the U.S. government

20. All of the following contribute to the trade deficit <u>except</u>:

   a. reduced production and labor costs among major U.S. manufacturing companies
   b. reduced labor and production costs in countries other than the U.S.
   c. restrictions on the importation of U.S.made products overseas
   d. the increased buying power of the U.S. dollar in the international market

21. The first federal legislation established to protect U.S workers in industry was:

   a. The Hamilton Act
   b. The Occupational Safety and Health Act
   c. The Sherman Anti-Trust Act
   d. The Federal Coal Mine Health and Safety Act

22. Those employed in U.S. sweatshops are most likely to be:

   a. Hispanic Americans
   b. Asian Americans
   c. illegal aliens
   d. all of the above

✓ 23. This theory maintains that a society is composed of equally powerful interest groups which direct policy.

   a. dialectical theory
   b. pluralist perspective
   c. elitist model
   d. consensual model

24. The Constitution established a system of ______________________ ______to insure no office would dominate the government.

a. debt and credit
b. executive and judicial branch
c. checks and balances
d. equity and fairness

25. Which of the following was an important factor in the transition from decentralized to centralized government in the U.S.?

a. the growth of the federal bureaucracy
b. an isolationist trade policy
c. a significant decline in the U.S. population following the Civil War
d. conflict between the federal government and individual states

26. The U.S. federal deficit:

a. doubled in the 1980s
b. was significantly cut in the 1980s
c. is not a major concern to U.S. policy-makers
d. can be paid for by trade surpluses of the 1980s

27. Political Action Committees (PACs) are most likely to give money to:

a. women
b. incumbents
c. new candidates
d. none of the above

28. The gender gap:

a. has not played a role in presidential politics
b. revolves around environmental, social welfare and foreign policy issues
c. is not valid as men and women vote similarly
d. played an important role the political process in the 1980's

29. Women and minorities have recently made the most significant inroads in:

a. state legislative seats
b. House of Representatives
c. Senate
d. all of the above

30. One of the most serious structural problems facing the Supreme Court is:

   a. the Justices have limited power because they must constantly campaign for re-appointment
   b. the Justices must hear every appeal of a State Supreme Court ruling
   c. the Court normally reinforces lower court rulings
   d. the Court can hear relatively few cases each year

31. Professionals hired by special interest groups to urge legislators to pass or defeat certain bills are known as:

   a. gerrymanders
   b. Political Action Committees
   c. representatives
   d. lobbyists

32. The creation of a federal law:

   a. requires the input of the Senate, House and President
   b. is a relatively quick process
   c. occurs only in the Senate with the approval of the President
   d. is carried out by the Supreme Court

33. The U.S. first emerged as a major military power during:

   a. the Revolutionary War
   b. World War I
   c. World War II
   d. the Persian Gulf conflict

34. Defense contractors:

   a. have significantly overcharged the government at times
   b. must estimate the total cost of a project before a contract is signed
   c. have never been found in violation of their contracts
   d. must absorb any cost-overruns

✓
35. All of the following are aspects of the military-industrial complex <u>except:</u>

   a. cost-overrun
   b. defense-dependence
   c. free competition among contractors
   d. exchange of personnel between the government and industry

36. Which of the following is not known as a federal "intelligence agency"?

    a. the National Security Council
    b. the National Reconnaissance Office
    c. the Central Intelligence Agency
    d. the Federal Bureau of Intelligence

37. Research indicates that in 1990, the major seller of arms to developing nations was:

    a. the Soviet Union
    b. China
    c. Lebanon
    d. the United States

38. The Gulf War resulted in:

    a. a "clean win" for the allied troops
    b. a large amount of Iraqi casualties
    c. environmental hazards for civilians
    d. all of the above

39. Historically, those countries allied with the United States were members of:

    a. the Warsaw Pact
    b. the U.S. Trust Resolution
    c. the North Atlantic Treaty Organization
    d. the United Nations

40. U.S. assistance to developing nations:

    a. results in guaranteed progress for the recipients
    b. results in equal distribution of the given resources among the recipient population
    c. is often used as a political tool
    d. none of the above

Fill in the Blanks

1. The Service sector of the U.S. economy currently employs the largest number of workers.

2. The legislation passed by Congress in 1970 which protects laborers in all U.S. industries, is known as the OHSA occupational Health & Safety Act.

3. An oligopoly occurs when a few companies control a particular market.

4. The close ties between defense contractors and the government is known as the Military-Industrial complex.

5. A member of the Supreme Court is appointed "for life or good behavior."

Matching

S 1. type of service sector job which includes education and health care
R 2. when a nation imports more than it exports
T 3. vertical merger
P 4. type of service sector job which includes cleaner and waitress
O 5. the system for the management and development of a society's resources
Q 6. lobbying groups who have powerful effects on elections
J 7. the largest supplier of nuclear arms to Third World Nations in the late 1980's
A 8. It's members are appointed for life or good behavior
E 9. consensus
F 10. the largest employer in the U.S.
H 11. when foreign investment exceeds a country's investment in foreign countries
G 12. inflation
C 13. executive branch
D 14. Oligopoly
I 15. $4.25 an hour
K 16. judicial branch
L 17. legislative branch
B 18. cost-overrun
M 19. NATO
N 20. arms race

A. Supreme Court
B. when the cost of a product exceeds the estimated cost
C. has the power to nominate Supreme Court members
D. another word for shared monopoly
E. another word for patterned pricing

F. service industry
G. economic indicator
H. debt crisis
I. minimum wage
J. the Soviet Union
K. reviews laws to ensure constitutionality
L. only federal officials directly elected by the people
M. indicated the countries aligned with the U.S.
N. the escalation of conventional and nuclear weaponry
O. economy
P. poverty service
Q. PAC
R. trade deficit
S. welfare jobs
T. when one company buys another in some way related to the former's production process

ANSWERS FOR CHAPTER 2

True/False

1.	False	21.	True
2.	True	22.	True
3.	False	23.	True
4.	True	24.	False
5.	True	25.	False
6.	False	26.	False
7.	False	27.	True
8.	False	28.	True
9.	True	29.	True
10.	False	30.	True
11.	True	31.	True
12.	False	32.	True
13.	False	33.	False
14.	True	34.	False
15.	True	35.	True
16.	False	36.	False
17.	False	37.	True
18.	True	38.	False
19.	False	39.	False
20.	False	40.	True

Multiple Choice

1.	d	21.	b
2.	a	22.	d
3.	d	23.	d
4.	c	24.	c

5.	d	25.	a
6.	b	26.	a
7.	d	27.	b
8.	c	28.	d
9.	d	29.	d
10.	b	30.	d
11.	d	31.	d
12.	c	32.	b
13.	d	33.	b
14.	d	34.	a
15.	b	35.	c
16.	d	36.	d
17.	a	37.	a
18.	b	38.	d
19.	c	39.	c
20.	a	40.	c

Fill in the Blanks

1. Service
2. Occupational Health and Safety Act
3. oligopoly
4. Military-industrial complex
5. Supreme Court

Matching

1. S
2. R
3. T
4. P
5. O
6. Q
7. J
8. A
9. E
10. F
11. H
12. G
13. C
14. D
15. I
16. K
17. L
18. B
19. M
20. N

CHAPTER 3

This chapter examines the problems of social class inequity and poverty on both a global scale and within the U.S. The conditions of developing countries are compared to those of the most advanced industrialized countries. The U.S. is characterized by a serous maldistribution of resources with the wealthy few holding the most resources. Poverty in the U.S. is closely examined as is the government's response to poverty.

A. GLOBAL INEQUALITY

Measuring inequality on a world scale proves difficult for several reasons. Income distribution among industrialized, developing and under-developed nations does offer some insight into the degree of inequality present in the world.

1. Some standardized measures are used to compare nations relative degree of inequality. However, these measures may be deceptive because they in themselves fail to reveal the differing impact they have on the nation in question.
2. One result of the unequal distribution of resources in the world is hunger or food shortages.
    a. Upon closer examination, it becomes apparent that the factors which contribute to food shortages result not from temporary trends of nature but more often from primitive farming methods, rapid population growth, and the political environment both internally and internationally.

b. Recent developments in the areas of health, education, and technology are discussed.

c. Some suggestions for ending world hunger such as relief aid, are assessed.

B. INEQUALITY IN THE U.S.

U.S. society is characterized by structural inequality and this section provides a profile of this inequality.

1. This section examines both income and wealth distribution in the U.S. over time which reveals a persistent trend in U.S. history; namely, the top few control the vast majority of wealth and income. This appears to be a structural reality.

2. Two models of social class are discussed.

   a. To aid us in understanding the concept of class, Weber identified three elements of social class: wealth, status, and power.

   b. The conflict perspective holds that class is determined by one's relationship to the means of production. According to this theory there are 3 classes in U.S. society: the wealthy, middle class, and the poor.

3. This section explores the disparate effects of taxes on these classes and the ability of the wealthy to maintain their position of power. We see how the distribution of economic resources contributes to the widening gap between "haves" and "have nots."

4. The "middle class" is defined and the variability of those included in this class is addressed.

C. POVERTY IN THE U.S.

Despite the fact that the U.S. is one of the wealthiest nations in the world, a large segment of its population lives in poverty.

1. The realities of poverty in the U.S. are addressed beginning with a discussion of who exactly constitutes "the poor."

    a. The most generally accepted measure of poverty in the U.S. is the poverty line or three times the cost of obtaining a minimally nutritious diet. This measurement has been criticized extensively on several grounds including: the diet used is for subsistence, not long-term nutrition; the ratio of food to non-food expenses has changed, pre-tax income is used; the process by which the poverty line is adjusted for inflation, indexing, does not ensure a fair standard of living. All these factors considered together translate into a dramatic under-estimation of the number of poor in the U.S.

    b. Stereotypes of the poor are contrasted with empirical evidence to show the facts about who constitutes the "underclass."

2. Two theoretical explanations of poverty are addressed.

    a. Theories of personal inferiority see poverty as the result of innate or natural weaknesses of the poor themselves.

    b. Theories of cultural inferiority hold that the poor have values and beliefs that differ from "mainstream" society and that the poor are unable to defer gratification.

3. Theories of structural poverty focus on society rather than the individual for an explanation of poverty.
   a. Proponents of functionalism claim that an unequal distribution of resources is necessary for the maintenance of society.
   b. Conflict theorists hold that society fails to provide more powerless groups with adequate education, employment or assistance.

D. GOVERNMENTAL EFFORTS TO REDUCE POVERTY

This section addresses the efforts which the federal government has made to combat the problem of poverty.

1. Government responses to poverty over the past fifty years, beginning with the New Deal Programs and including the 1960s War on Poverty are evaluated. The assumptions behind these programs--e.g. that poverty is a short term problem and that full employment is a feasible goal--are criticized.
2. Crucial changes in assistance programs which occurred during the Reagan/Bush years such as cutting funds and stricter guidelines for programs are discussed. The impact of these cuts into the 1990s are assessed.
3. The federal policy towards the poor during the 1990's is addressed. Particular attention is given to the 1994 "Contract with America" which calls for a "crackdown on welfare."

SELF-TEST

True/False

1. Income inequality is most commonly measured by the distribution of income and wealth.

   a. true
   b. false

2. Regardless of the state of development, inequality between quintiles is extreme.

   a. true
   b. false

3. Compared to other industrialized nations, in the U.S. there is little difference between the amount of income earned by those in the lowest and highest quintiles.

   a. true
   b. false

4. Population growth of underdeveloped countries a whole will be less than industrialized countries in the next decade.

   a. true
   b. false

5. The only way to accurately compare world inequality is by examining each country's GNP.

   a. true
   b. false

6. "Subsistence level" production best describes how the majority of underdeveloped nations produce food.

   a. true
   b. false

7. Half of the world's population lives in underdeveloped countries.

   a. true
   b. false

8. The U.S. has the lowest infant mortality rate in the world.

   a. true
   b. false

9. According to Earthscan, famine cannot be prevented ahead of time.

a. true
b. false

10. Relief in the form of food and supplies for famine victims is considered to be a short-term solution to the famine problem.

a. true
b. false

11. Wealth refers to the total amount of income an individual receives for one year.

a. true
b. false

12. In the U.S. there is an equitable distribution of income.

a. true
b. false

13. The richest one percent of the U.S. population controls one quarter of the nation's wealth.

a. true
b. false

14. A member of the upper-lower class would be considered a professional.

a. true
b. false

15. The "wealthy" are best described as those who have great power in society because of their tremendous financial resources.

a. true
b. false

16. Conflict theorists focus on eduction as the most important determinant of class.

a. true
b. false

17. Max Weber developed one of earliest conceptualizations of class.

a. true
b. false

18. Everyone in the U.S. is "functionally literate."

a. true
b. false

19. The overall female literacy rate in underdeveloped countries is much higher than the male rate.

a. true
b. false

20. Currently there are millions of millionaires in the U.S.

a. true
b. false

21. Data indicates that the tax burden in the U.S. is distributed "proportionately."

a. true
b. false

22. Trickle-down theory maintains that certain tax loopholes for corporations are negative for society in general.

a. true
b. false

23. The most significant loopholes in the federal tax system are found in corporate taxation.

a. true
b. false

24. Corporate contributions to the tax base make up over 50% of federal funding.

a. true
b. false

25. The power of the wealthy is an institutionalized part of our society.

a. true
b. false

26. The federal subsidization of the upper segment of the population is known as "wealthfare".

a. true
b. false

27. The working class in the corporate sector is generally organized through trade unions.

    a. true
    b. false

28. Generally managers wield more political power than professionals and blue-collar workers

    a. true
    b. false

29. The poverty line is generally accepted as establishing an accurate cut-off for determining welfare assistance.

    a. true
    b. false

30. It is estimated that if the poverty line were calculated accurately, the number of people included would decrease by 10%.

    a. true
    b. false

31. Most poor people are young, jobless, black and male.

    a. true
    b. false

32. The majority of "poor" adults are working or looking for work.

    a. true
    b. false

33. Herbert Spencer suggested that the poor are poor because they lack natural talents with which to succeed.

    a. true
    b. false

34. Functionalists believe that inequality is dysfunctional and plays no significant role in society.

    a. true
    b. false

35. Conflict theorists argue that the poor are poor as a result of structural inequality.

a. true
b. false

36. The "War on Poverty" was initially launched in the 1930s.

a. true
b. false

37. Only a small segment of the population was affected by the Great Depression.

a. true
b. false

38. The number of poor people decreased in the 1980s.

a. true
b. false

39. Studies indicate that even when they combine maximum welfare payments, poor people must often work to bring their income up to the poverty line.

a. true
b. false

40. The Reagan administration was instrumental in providing more benefits to the poor.

a. true
b. false

Multiple Choice

1. The term __________ refers to all assets including stocks, bonds, money and property.

a. income
b. wealth
c. inequity
d. market

2. Which of the following is <u>not</u> a category of development as specified by the World Bank?

   a. low-income economy
   b. lower-middle income economy
   c. high income economy
   d. nonmarket economy

3. When we rank all households according to annual incomes and then separate them into five equal parts from the lowest to the highest, we are creating:

   a. inequality
   b. quintiles
   c. categories
   d. none of the above

4. The "slash and burn" technique:

   a. eventually depletes the soil of minerals
   b. is used to clear forests
   c. has recently been created in undeveloped countries
   d. does not provide suitable areas for growing

5. The famine in Ethiopia:

   a. came about completely unexpectedly
   b. received complete government attention and resources
   c. was seen as a minor problem by the U.N.
   d. was exacerbated by governmental policies

6. All of the following are basic indicators of a country's living standard <u>except:</u>

   a. GNP
   b. life expectancy at birth
   c. infant mortality
   d. population per dentist

7. Currently we see the highest population growth in:

   a. industrialized countries
   b. advanced nonmarket nations
   c. Third World countries
   d. none of the above--all countries have low growth rates

8. Inequality among different nations exists in the form of:

   a. economic inequality
   b. educational inequality
   c. unequal health care
   d. all of the above

9. The most striking advances in developing countries in recent years have been in the area of:

   a. industrialization
   b. adult literacy
   c. life expectancy
   d. farming technology

10. If we examine the distribution of income in the United States over the past 50 years, we notice:

   a. there has been a definite trend in a redistribution of the wealth
   b. the wealth of those in the lowest quintile is rapidly increasing
   c. the income distribution has remained relatively constant
   d. none of the above

11. The richest one percent of U.S citizens control:

   a. one percent of the nation's wealth
   b. more than 50% of the nation's wealth
   c. their equitable share of the nation's wealth
   d. one quarter of the nation's wealth

12. The most reliable variables used to distinguish class:

   a. are power and wealth
   b. are dress and education
   c. have not yet been found
   d. do not vary from culture to culture

13. Max Weber included three elements in his description of class. Which of the following is not one of them?

   a. wealth
   b. status
   c. power
   d. education

14. Sociologists working from the conflict perspective examine class as determined by one's relationship to:

a. others who are well educated
b. the means of production
c. others who are wealthy
d. parental status

15. ____________________ identified three basic classes, each having two subdivisions.

a. Max Weber
b. Karl Marx
c. Emile Durkheim
d. William Lloyd Warner

16. The tax system during the Reagan administration:

a. granted substantial tax breaks to major corporations
b. significantly cut the enormous profits of top companies
c. did not change how corporations were taxed
d. increased revenues for the federal government from prior years

17. Conflict theorists argue that the relationship between one's economic position and education, lifestyle, dress and so on, is:

a. reciprocal
b. nonexistent
c. proportional
d. all of the above

18. Which of the following is <u>not</u> a reason for the lack of formal education within Third World nations.

a. lack of governmental funding
b. lack of qualified teachers
c. lack of interest among the people, especially women
d. difficulty in developing schools in rural areas

19. In the U.S., the one area in which the elite <u>do not</u> exert power disproportionately is:

a. the political arena
b. the corporate arena
c. the legislative arena
d. none of the above; the elite are powerful in each

20. The type of taxation which proposes that as one's income increases, so does the percentage of taxes one is expected to pay, is known as:

a. regressive tax
b. progressive tax
c. proportional tax
d. trickle-down

21. The argument that liberal tax expenditures will help economic growth and benefit the average person, is known as:

a. the welfare system
b. tax expenditure theory
c. trickle-down theory
d. loop-hole theory

22. Which of the following is <u>not</u> a form of tax break?

a. exclusions
b. deductions
c. capital gains
d. tax sheltering

23. Loopholes in the federal tax system most clearly benefit:

a. the wealthy
b. the poor
c. corporations
d. both a and c above

24. In the U.S., most people characterize themselves as:

a. upper class
b. middle class
c. working class
d. lower class

25. Which of the following is <u>not</u> a member of the middle class, given your text's definition?

a. a physician
b. a manager
c. a college professor
d. a factory owner

26. According to the text, the criteria used for determining the middle class are that one does not live below the poverty line, and:

a. does not own the means of production
b. is a professional
c. works in a blue collar job
d. has a college degree

27. The federally established poverty line:

a. is three times the cost of obtaining a minimally nutritional diet
b. was developed by studying the spending habits of the upper class
c. has not met with substantive criticisms
d. has improved through objective methods

28. Which of the following is a common critique of the poverty line?

a. it overestimates the number of impoverished people
b. people spend more than 1/3 of their income on food
c. the line over-adjusts for inflation
d. the diet used as the basic measurement fails to meet the nutritional needs of the poor over time

29. Individuals whose incomes hover around the poverty line are known as:

a. truly poor
b. middle-class
c. near-poor
d. all of the above

30. If measured appropriately, it is estimated that the number of people living in poverty in the U.S. would be:

a. 5 million
b. 25 million
c. 50 million
d. 100 million

31. The underclass in the U.S.:

a. is primarily African American
b. lives primarily in the inner-city
c. receives welfare
d. none of the above

32. Which of the following groups are disproportionately represented among the poor?

a. African Americans
b. female heads of households
c. children
d. all of the above

33. Poverty has been attributed to:

a. mental and emotional deficiencies
b. the influence of the Roman Catholic church
c. the failed attempt to implement Marxist principles of economics into the U.S.
d. widespread acceptance of the beliefs of Sigmund Freud

34. This theory maintains that the poor as a group possess values and goals which differ from the rest of the population, and perpetuate their poverty.

a. Personal Inferiority
b. Psychological Deficiency
c. Cultural Inferiority
d. Circle of Destitution

35. A functionalist approach to poverty:

a. states that the poor are useless and parasitical
b. advocates the use of sterilization on the poor
c. seeks to restructure the social system to put an end to poverty
d. believes that the poor are useful in that they can perform dirty, menial jobs

36. Which of the following does not rely on a structural view of poverty?

a. William Julius Wilson
b. Michael Harrington
c. Oscar Lewis
d. all of the above

37. The Great Depression in the 1930s:

a. ushered in a series of social reform programs
b. only affected a small and mostly immigrant portion of the population
c. caused unemployment to rise to over 50%
d. was the most prosperous time in U.S. history

38. Welfare programs in the U.S. were developed:

a. to benefit the middle and upper classes
b. to allow "handouts" for needy citizens
c. with long-term goals in mind
d. with a "band-aid" mentality

39. Recent changes in federal assistance to the poor include:

a. increases in the number of people entitled to food stamps
b. increases in funding for the CETA program
c. increases in rent for federally subsidized low-income housing
d. increasing payments of Aid to Families with Dependent Children

40. Following the 1994 elections, there was

a. an increase in funding to poor families with children
b. a $40 million increase to food and housing programs for the poor
c. a "crackdown on welfare"
d. no significant changes to eliminating poverty in the U.S

Fill in the Blanks.

1. Social class is the measure of one's economic position in society.

2. The trickle-Down theory maintains that tax-breaks given to the wealthy will translate into increased job opportunities for the average person.

3. The two major theoretical explanations for poverty are cultural inferiority and STRUCTURAL.

4. The Near Poor are often denied public assistance despite their genuine need.

5. The tendency to evaluate one's economic situation in terms of one's own society is known as Relitive deperivation.

Matching

1. N The tendency to evaluate other countries' social, political, or economic situation in terms of one's own social group.
2. D the core
3. E the periphery
4. B liberal tax expenditures
5. H when an equal proportion of taxes is assessed at all income levels
6. L when those with less money spend a greater proportion of their income on taxes than those with more money
7. P as an individual's income increases, so does his/her tax bracket
8. M When your income hovers around the poverty line
9. I three times a nutritionally balanced diet--thrifty food plan
10. A Oscar Lewis
11. C <u>The Bell Curve</u> Charles Murry
12. F <u>The Other America</u> Micheal Harrington
13. Q <u>The Truly Disadvantaged</u> William Julius Wilson
14. G first divided class into three categories, each with three subdivisions Lloyd WARNER
15. J made the classic statement on social class MAX weber
16. R wealth total assets
17. T middle-class near-poor & people who don't control production
18. K GNP WORLD BANK uses to catatorize development
19. O wealth distribution
20. S upper-upper class

A. culture of poverty
B. loop-holes
C. Charles Murray
D. industrialized countries
E. underdeveloped countries
F. Michael Harrington
G. Lloyd Warner
H. proportional tax
I. official poverty line
J. Max Weber
K. the World Bank uses this statistic to categorize countries at different stages of development
L. regressive tax
M. near-poor
N. relative deprivation
O. the manner in which all assets are distributed throughout a society
P. progressive tax
Q. William Julius Wilson
R. total assets possessed by an individual or family
S. the established wealth of the U.S. with high society life-styles
T. includes the non-poor and those who don't own the means of production

ANSWERS TO CHAPTER 3

True/False

1.	True	21.	True
2.	True	22.	False
3.	False	23.	True
4.	False	24.	False
5.	False	25.	True
6.	True	26.	True
7.	True	27.	True
8.	False	28.	False
9.	False	29.	False
10.	True	30.	False
11.	False	31.	False
12.	False	32.	True
13.	True	33.	True
14.	False	34.	False
15.	True	35.	True
16.	False	36.	False
17.	True	37.	False
18.	False	38.	False
19.	False	39.	True
20.	True	40.	False

Multiple Choice

1.	b	21.	c
2.	d	22.	c
3.	b	23.	d
4.	a	24.	b
5.	d	25.	d
6.	d	26.	a
7.	c	27.	a
8.	d	28.	d
9.	c	29.	c
10.	c	30.	c
11.	d	31.	d
12.	a	32.	d
13.	d	33.	a
14.	b	34.	c
15.	d	35.	d
16.	a	36.	c
17.	a	37.	a
18.	c	38.	d
19.	d	39.	c
20.	b	40.	c

Fill in the Blanks

1. Social class
2. Trickle-down theory
3. Structural
4. Near poor
5. Relative Deprivation

Matching

1. N
2. D
3. E
4. B
5. H
6. L
7. P
8. M
9. I
10. A
11. C
12. F
13. Q
14. G
15. J
16. R
17. T
18. K
19. O
20. S

CHAPTER 4

This chapter examines the racial and ethnic problems prevalent in the United States both historically and today. Recent years have seen both an increase in bias crimes and increased racial tensions. In contrast, some racial and ethnic groups appear to be making progress. The experiences of African Americans, Native Americans, Asian Americans, and Hispanic Americans are discussed in detail along with several theories of race and ethnic relations.

A. ETHNICITY, RACE AND MINORITY GROUP STATUS

Some basic definitions are clarified in this chapter.

1. For the purpose of this chapter, an ethnic group is defined as a group whose members share a common cultural heritage.
2. Race is a more illusive category to define since racial categories and definitions vary cross culturally. Race is defined as a social creation based on perceived biological characteristics.
3. Although prejudice and discrimination are related, prejudice deals with attitudes, while discrimination deals with actions.
4. Institutional discrimination in many cases acts to preserve and legitimize discriminatory practices within societies and operates to systematically deny powerless groups equal access to opportunities and resources.

B. ASSESSING THE IMPACT OF INSTITUTIONAL DISCRIMINATION: FOUR EXAMPLES

In order to examine institutional discrimination in the United States, four groups are identified and examined in detail.

1. African Americans have a unique history of oppression and segregation in the United States. This history is traced from the days of slavery, through the post Civil War reforms and to the Civil Rights movement of the 1960s. Gains of the 1960s as well as setbacks of the 1970s and 1980s are discussed.
    a. African Americans still have lower economic status as a group compared to whites. Recently, statistical evidence shows that their economic condition is deteriorating. Specific indicators discussed are income, wealth, unemployment, and percentage of the population living in poverty.
    b. African Americans have achieved increased political representation, primarily on the state and local levels. Important to note, however, is the declining percentage of African Americans in higher education.
    c. Discrimination is not only faced by the underclass, but by African-Americans of all classes.
2. Native Americans have been largely ignored throughout U.S. history. Due to their systematic oppression by the federal government, this group merits special attention.
    a. Ethnocentricity and homogeneity of Europeans fueled feelings of racial superiority and characterized the federal government's treatment of Native Americans. Violation of contracts or treaties and forced reallocation were common tactics.

b. Although Native Americans have won several important legal and political battles, they continue to be a highly disadvantaged group. Today unemployment rates for Native Americans are among the highest in the nation. They have the lowest educational attainment of any U.S. minority group and also fare badly in the area of health, specifically in shorter life expectancy and higher infant mortality rates.

c. The conditions on Indian reservations are discussed and some reservations are likened to the economic situation in Third World countries.

3. Asian Americans have been referred to as the "model minority" primarily because of their higher than average educational attainment. The problematic implications of this assumption are presented.

a. The term "Asian" obscures the diversity of this group. Concrete historical examples are provided to illustrate the historical discrimination that has faced various subgroups, including the internment of U.S citizens of Japanese descent during World War II.

b. Recent Asian immigration experience including that of the Filipinos, Koreans, and Vietnamese is discussed in comparison to the experience of earlier groups.

c. Despite their high enrollment in higher education, Asian Americans represent only a small percentage of those in top ranking positions. In addition, the use of family income as an indicator of economic well-being obscures the earning ability of individual members. The stereotype of Asian Americans as "hardworking" operates to exclude many from receiving assistance.

4. Demographers have predicted that Hispanic Americans, the second fastest growing minority in the U.S., will displace African Americans as the largest minority by 2020.

   a. Although many economic indicators suggest that Hispanic Americans are better off, on the whole, than African Americans, they lag significantly behind whites particularly in terms of educational achievement and employment.

   b. Hispanic Americans also represent a diverse group. The experiences of Chicanos, the largest group of Hispanics in the U.S is highlighted.

   c. The 1980s and 1990s have seen a renewed commitment to limiting illegal immigration. The primary target of stricter laws are Mexican Americans. Critics of these measures argue that they operate to drive further underground the use of illegal immigrants as cheap labor and discriminate against legal immigrants.

C. THE INTERNATIONAL DIMENSION OF RACISM

Obviously, racism is not a problem limited to U.S. society. Some of the more infamous examples of racism are provided such as Nazi Germany, Amin's Uganda, and Pol Pot's Cambodia.

1. One area that has recently received worldwide attention for its

institutionalized legally-enforced system of segregation and oppression based on race is South Africa. The protests of Native Blacks as well as international sanctions are evaluated. The effectiveness of sanctions, especially disinvestment has been questioned, and the consequences of the formal repeal of apartheid are assessed.

2. Eastern and Central Europe are also discussed with regard to the widespread civil war and practices of "ethnic cleansing" in countries such as Bosnia and Romania.

D. EXPLAINING RACISM

In an effort to understand racism, sociologists have forwarded varying explanations.

1. The primordialist perspective views racial and ethnic identification as a basic element of human nature. The preference for one's "own kind" is innate as is the disdain for differing groups. Criticisms of this perspective are presented in detail.
2. Those who are dissatisfied with the primordialist perspective claim that racism is rooted in social causes. Socialization is a factor that cannot be underestimated in evaluating racial identifications and prejudices. Solutions forwarded include encouraging pluralism or promoting assimilation.
3. Conflict theorists agree that the causes of racial stratification are social in nature, however, they argue that assimilation devalues minority cultures and places responsibility on members of disadvantaged groups. Also, they question the value of

interaction among groups unless the groups have equal status. Conflict theorists favor the pluralist model. They feel that racism results from competition in a society for scarce resources and an unequal distribution of power. An analysis of historical trends supports this, since racial tension increases during periods of economic decline.

SELF-TEST

True/False

1. Since the 1960s, we have seen almost the total elimination of residential segregation in the U.S.

   a. true
   b. false

2. The National Institute Against Prejudice and Violence estimates that less than 5% of minority group members are the victims of hate crimes each year.

   a. true
   b. false

3. College campuses remain one of the few places devoid of bias crimes.

   a. true
   b. false

4. Ethnicity is an identification with one's "own kind of people," according to sociologists.

   a. true
   b. false

5. Differences between ethnic groups are primarily biological in nature.

   a. true
   b. false

6. The Burakumin of Japan are highly respected members of society.

   a. true
   b. false

7. The importance of skin color as a determinant of racial heritage varies cross-culturally.

   a. true
   b. false

8. Minority group status deals primarily with the groups' numerical representation in a society.

   a. true
   b. false

9. Almost every racial/ethnic group in U.S. society has been stereotyped at one time or another.

   a. true
   b. false

10. If one discriminates, one is always prejudiced.

   a. true
   b. false

11. Institutional discrimination is much less harmful to a society and individuals than "individual discrimination."

   a. true
   b. false

12. Cuban Americans came to the U.S. largely as middle and upper-middle class professionals.

   a. true
   b. false

13. Jim Crow laws allowed African Americans to integrate into society after the Civil War.

   a. true
   b. false

14. The Thirteenth Amendment abolished slavery.

   a. true
   b. false

15. After Emancipation, African Americans were still treated unequally relative to whites in terms of voting rights and job opportunities.

   a. true
   b. false

16. The Plessy vs. Ferguson decision ruled that racially segregated schools were unconstitutional.

    a. true
    b. false

17. In 1992, Carol Moseley Brown became the first elected African American governor.

    a. true
    b. false

18. The 1964 Civil Rights Act prohibited employment discrimination on the basis of race.

    a. true
    b. false

19. Over the last five years, African Americans have made significant advances in national and state politics.

    a. true
    b. false

20. In the early 1990's, the percentage of African Americans living in poverty was slightly higher than whites.

    a. true
    b. false

21. Homicide is the leading cause of death among African American males aged 15-24.

    a. true
    b. false

22. African American teenagers are just as likely to be employed as white teenagers.

    a. true
    b. false

23. African American children are three times as likely as white children to live in poverty.

    a. true
    b. false

24. The highest percentage of families with children under the age of 18 and living in poverty are headed by single African American men.

   a. true
   b. false

25. Sociological research indicates that it is only the African American underclass which suffers discrimination--not the middle class.

   a. true
   b. false

26. In recent years we have seen a growing economic gap between middle class African Americans and the underclass.

   a. true
   b. false

27. Prior to colonization, Native American tribes were quite similar in their cultures and thus, homogeneous.

   a. true
   b. false

28. The "Right of Discovery" granted first legal jurisdiction over a territory to the first European nation with an established settlement.

   a. true
   b. false

29. Many Native Americans were denied the right to vote until the 1940s.

   a. true
   b. false

30. The plan of "termination" set out to make the Indian reservation system autonomous and to encourage tribal customs.

   a. true
   b. false

31. The primary reason for Native Americans' low level of educational attainment is disinterest in schooling.

   a. true
   b. false

32. Asian Americans have been called the "model minority" because of their economic and educational success.

a. true
b. false

33. Japanese-Americans were excluded from fighting with the U.S. armed forces during World War II.

a. true
b. false

34. In 1882, the U.S. government eliminated any exclusionary practices against Chinese immigration.

a. true
b. false

35. Every group of Asian Americans has met with similar economic and educational success.

a. true
b. false

36. Hispanic Americans are the slowest growing minority group in the U.S.

a. true
b. false

37. Illegal immigrants in the U.S. come only from Mexico and other Latin American countries.

a. true
b. false

38. Unlike other minority group members, Mexican Americans have rapidly entered professional occupations as a result of their educational achievements.

a. true
b. false

39. In 1992, Nelson Mandela was elected the first black president of South Africa.

a. true
b. false

40. Historical evidence indicates that racial hostility grows during periods of economic decline.

a. true
b. false

Multiple Choice

1. Most studies indicate that in recent years, bias crimes:

a. are increasing
b. are decreasing
c. have been eliminated
d. have ceased to be labelled a "social problem"

2. Currently, racial violence is committed most frequently by:

a. members of heavy metal rock groups
b. people under 30 years old
c. people between 30 and 50 years of age
d. none of the above

3. A group whose members share a common cultural heritage that they pass on from one generation to the next is called:

a. a race
b. burakumin
c. an ethnic group
d. ethnocentrism

4. _________ is a social creation based on perceived biological differences between groups of people.

a. ethnicity
b. race
c. burakumin
d. culture

5. Racial categories are created when individuals:

a. share a common skin, hair, and eye color
b. share a common moral character
c. share a common mentality
d. define themselves as physically different from others, and act on these differences

6. Racism is:

a. the unjust treatment of a group of people on the basis of their race
b. the classification of races according to specific biological criteria
c. the shared cultural heritage of a racial group
d. a distinction between groups that are clearly physically different from one another

7. Minority groups:

a. always constitute the numerical minority in a society
b. are always considered to be biologically inferior to the majority group
c. have less power than the majority group
d. all of the above

8. Denying a group of people access to society's resources and rewards is:

a. prejudice
b. stereotyping
c. cultural relativism
d. discrimination

9. An attribute of one's identity which takes on the most important significance to others is:

a. a stereotype
b. a master status
c. primary status
d. racism

10. "Prejudice" refers to biased __________, whereas "discrimination" refers to biased ___________.

a. behavior, stereotyping
b. actions, beliefs
c. beliefs, actions
d. none of the above

11. When the elements of the social structure systematically disadvantage particular groups, this is known as:

a. structural racism
b. ethnocentrism
c. institutional prejudice
d. institutional discrimination

12. Which of the following is a direct form of institutional discrimination?

    a. genocide
    b. expulsion
    c. exclusion
    d. all of the above

13. The form of institutionalized discrimination in which a group is forcibly removed from an area is called:

    a. exclusion
    b. expulsion
    c. genocide
    d. infanticide

14. Which group has the highest unemployment rate in the U.S.?

    a. African American
    b. Hispanic American
    c. Native American
    d. Asian American

15. __________ have the highest high-school drop out rate in this society.

    a. African Americans
    b. Hispanic Americans
    c. Native Americans
    d. Asian Americans

16. The largest Hispanic American group in the U.S. is

    a. Puerto Rican
    b. Mexican American
    c. Dominican Republican American
    d. Cuban

17. Slavery was abolished with:

    a. the Reconstruction Amendments
    b. the Thirteenth Amendment
    c. the Fourteenth Amendment
    d. the Fifteenth Amendment

18. The Supreme Court decision that declared the principle of "separate but equal" unconstitutional was:

a. Brown v. Board of Education
b. Plessy v. Ferguson
c. Roe v. Wade
d. Bowers v. Hardwick

19. Proposition 187, passed in California

a. increased the number of Mexicans legally allowed in the U.S
b. harshly sanctioned discrimination against Mexican Americans
c. denied health care and schooling to undocumented immigrants
d. allowed for a one year amnesty period for illegal aliens to prove they have lived for a significant time in the U.S.

20. The _______ is known as the "golden age" for African Americans due to their great economic and political gains.

a. 1890s
b. 1940s
c. 1950s
d. 1960s

21. The enfranchisement of African-Americans was effectively guaranteed with:

a. the Fourteenth Amendment
b. the Fifteenth Amendment
c. the 1964 Civil Rights Act
d. the 1965 Voter's Rights Act

22. In terms of educational advancement, African Americans are losing ground with regard to:

a. college completion rates
b. their representation in higher education
c. high school completion rates
d. all of the above

23. In recent years there has been a narrowing of the gap between African Americans and white Americans in:

a. educational attainment
b. life expectancy
c. infant mortality
d. median family income

24. With regard to economic advances, African Americans:

a. have a family income equal to whites
b. earn almost 90% of white per capita income
c. are increasing their numbers in the highest U.S. income bracket
d. are increasing their numbers in the lowest U.S. income bracket
e. both c and d

25. Studies indicate that African American workers are likely to be concentrated in which of the following jobs?

a. executive
b. technician
c. professional specialists
d. none of the above

26. Regardless of class, African Americans are still likely to experience:

a. residential segregation
b. higher rates of unemployment than whites
c. lower median incomes than whites with the same educational credentials
d. all of the above

27. ______________ are the only minority which currently has a government agency to govern its affairs exclusively.

a. African Americans
b. Cuban-Americans
c. Native Americans
d. Asian Americans

28. All of the following is true with regard to U.S. government policy towards Native Americans prior to the 20th century <u>except:</u>

a. Native Americans were prohibited from practicing their tribal customs
b. Native Americans were granted U.S. citizenship in 1871
c. Native Americans were forced to attend BIA boarding schools
d. all of the above are true

29. This program was instrumental in promoting Native American leadership and activism.

a. Johnson's "Great Society"
b. Roosevelt's "New Deal"
c. Bush's "Tribal Unity" program
d. none of the above

30. The racial minority group in the U.S. which suffers the poorest health and the lowest level of educational attainment is:

a. African Americans
b. Native Americans
c. Hispanic Americans
d. Asian Americans

31. Native American reservations are likely to:

a. have high levels of unemployment
b. have substandard housing conditions
c. exploit the natural resources of the reservation by setting up independent enterprises
d. all of the above are true
e. both a and b

32. Compared with white Americans, Asian Americans:

a. have a lower median income
b. have a higher average level of educational attainment
c. have a lower average level of educational attainment
d. are culturally homogeneous

33. Which racial minority is experiencing the most rapid growth?

a. Hispanic Americans
b. Native Americans
c. African-Americans
d. Asian Americans

34. The ____________ were the first Asians to emigrate to the U.S. in large numbers.

a. Vietnamese
b. Japanese
c. Chinese
d. Koreans

35. In 1942, of the 120,000 Japanese held in internment camps which of the following was <u>excluded?</u>

a. Japanese enemy aliens
b. resident Japanese aliens
c. U.S. citizens of Japanese descent
d. none of the above

36. This group has the lowest educational and occupational status among Asian Americans.

a. Chinese
b. Japanese
c. Koreans
d. Vietnamese

37. Compared to African Americans, Hispanic Americans are characterized by all of the following <u>except</u>:

a. a lower unemployment rate
b. a lower rate of poverty
c. a higher median income
d. a higher level of educational attainment

38. Relative to white Americans, Hispanic Americans:

a. have a higher unemployment rate
b. have a lower high school drop out rate
c. have a higher median family income
d. are wealthier if wealth is measured in overall earnings

39. A sociologist who emphasizes teaching children early on to respect racial and ethnic diversity may be said to be working from:

a. a primordialist perspective
b. a structural functionalist perspective
c. a cultural assimilationist perspective
d. a pluralist perspective

40. The emotional attachment of people to their own ethnic group in a multi-ethnic society is known as

a. ethnocentrism
b. ethnonationalism
c. ethnic-cleansing
d. racial elitism

Fill in the Blanks.

1. The term underclass refers to the already-disadvantaged who face chronic unemployment and poverty.

2. Over 4,000 Cherokee men, women and children died in the forced march of relocation known as Trail of Tears.

3. The Chinese Exclusion Act prohibited the immigration of Chinese between 1882 and 1943.

4. Mexican make up the most significant proportion of illegal immigrants in the U.S.

5. "The development of interdependence, appreciation, and the skills for interacting intimately with persons from other cultures" is known as Pluralism.

Matching

1. When members of a group share a common cultural heritage
2. When members of a group share a perceived genetic heritage
3. An oversimplified, summary description which applies to all members of a group
4. Actions which deny individuals equal access to society's rewards
5. The deliberate attempt to exterminate an entire race/ethnic group
6. The Supreme Court ruling that "separate but equal" was constitutional
7. The Supreme Court ruling that "separate but equal" was unconstitutional
8. an emotional attachment to members of one's own ethnic group in a multi-ethnic society
9. "Rights of Discovery"
10. highest rate of unemployment
11. highest high-school drop-out rate
12. middle minority
13. the first Asians to arrive in large numbers
14. most affluent Hispanic American group in the U.S.
15. the largest Hispanic American group in the U.S.
16. bracero program
17. racist practice implemented by the government of South Africa
18. when one develops an understanding and appreciation for racial and ethnic diversity
19. otherwise known as "the melting pot"
20. sees racism as a natural phenomenon

A. stereotype
B. genocide
C. Plessy v. Ferguson
D. ethnonationalism
E. African-Americans
F. ethnic group
G. Brown v. Board of Education
H. basically a policy of "finders keepers"
I. race
J. discrimination
K. Native Americans
L. Chinese
M. Mexican Americans
N. apartheid
O. primordialist perspective
P. federal program to bring in Mexicans as cheap labor
Q. assimilation
R. pluralism
S. Cubans
T. Asian Americans

ANSWERS TO CHAPTER 4

True/False

1. False
2. False
3. False
4. True
5. False
6. False
7. True
8. False
9. True
10. False
11. False
12. True
13. False
14. True
15. True
16. False
17. False
18. True
19. True
20. False
21. True
22. False
23. True
24. False
25. False
26. True
27. False
28. True
29. True
30. False
31. False
32. True
33. False
34. False
35. False
36. False
37. False
38. False
39. True
40. True

Multiple Choice

1. a
2. b
3. c
4. b
5. d
6. a
7. c
8. d
9. b
10. c
11. d
12. d
13. b
14. a
15. c
16. b
17. b
18. a
19. c
20. d
21. d
22. b
23. a
24. e
25. d
26. d
27. c
28. b
29. a
30. b
31. e
32. b
33. d
34. c
35. d
36. d
37. d
38. a
39. d
40. b

Fill in the Blanks

1. Underclass
2. Trail of Tears
3. Chinese Exclusion Act
4. Mexican
5. Pluralism

Matching

1. F
2. I
3. A
4. J
5. B
6. C
7. G
8. D
9. H
10. E
11. K
12. T
13. L
14. S
15. M
16. P
17. N
18. R
19. Q
20. O

CHAPTER 5

The United States is a society which is characterized by gender inequality and heterosexism. The prevalence of institutionalized gender inequality in the U.S. is examined in this chapter. The impact of this form of stratification and others, such as that based on equal orientation, is explored though a discussion of how the social construction of gender (in education, the media, and the workplace) shapes the life chances of men and women. This chapter also details the history and progress of the women's liberation movement and the gay rights movement.

A. SOCIOLOGICAL PERSPECTIVES ON GENDER AND SEXUAL ORIENTATION

Gender inequality stems from the creation of social categories (masculinity/femininity) called gender and their assignment based on one's biological sex. These social constructions create expectations for behavior that are embedded in social institutions. These institutionalized patterns of gender differentiation are referred to as a society's <u>sex/gender system</u>, which often results in social stratification. Although differences do exist between the sexes, sociologists continue to debate the extent to which these differences are biologically determined or are products of social learning and social control.

1. There are several different perspectives which seek to explain sex/gender systems.

a. According to <u>sociobiologists</u>, biological differences account for any observed differences in behavior. Men's and women's differing reproductive functions were said to suit them for different roles. This perspective implies that gender prescribed behavior is fixed and innate. Accompanying this assumption is one that deems conformity to one's gender role as correct and non-conformity as deviant.

b. Beginning in the early 1990's, there has been increasing debate about the connection between genetic or biological mutation and homosexuality. This evidence is reviewed and critiqued.

c. The <u>feminist perspective</u> maintains that gender is a socially created set of expectations, transmitted through socialization. Although biology does establish limits for our behavior, these limits are broad and in no way determine behavior.

   1. The maintenance of a sex-gender system requires more than socialization; it also requires a political and socio-economic structure that supports the system.
   2. Through cross-cultural and cross-historical research, proponents of the feminist perspective have discovered a variety of sex-gender systems, which further supports the claim that sex-gender systems are social constructions.

B. THE STATUS OF WOMEN AND MEN IN CONTEMPORARY SOCIETY

The U.S. is characterized by a patriarchal sex/gender system which has implications for both men and women at all levels of society.

1. The media is a powerful agent of socialization which often reinforces gender stereotypes. The <u>reflection hypothesis</u> is often used to explain this trend, but the media also <u>creates</u> culture.
   a. The media have frequently been accused of the symbolic annihilation of women, both explicitly and implicitly.
   b. Newspapers have a tradition of portraying women's news as "soft-news" and underrepresenting women on the front-page.
   c. The reinforcement of gender, racial, and homosexual stereotypes on prime-time television is discussed.
2. Title IX has been successful in eliminating the most blatant forms of gender inequality in our nations' schools. However studies continue to document ways in which teachers treat students differently on the basis of sex.
   a. It has been argued that boys' higher achievement in some subjects reflects a natural ability. However, these abilities develop over time, therefore, it is doubtful that these abilities are innate.
   b. The factors which contribute to the aspirations of students are presented.
   c. Although women make up the majority of those

students attending college, they still continue to experience discrimination and inequality.

3. A brief review of women's role in the labor force over time establishes the fact that women have been used as a pool of reserve labor to be used as needed, and then dismissed.

   a. Although the percentage of women participating in the labor force has increased dramatically, the labor force is still characterized by occupational sex segregation.

   b. The persistence of this phenomenon is due to the weakness of the legislation meant to alleviate this disparity. In addition, stereotypes have led employers to value "women's work" less than "men's work."

   c. It has been argued that women choose different occupations than men. One explanation for this, Human Capital Theory is discussed and critiqued.

C. JUSTICE FOR ALL?

Traditionally gays and lesbians have been denied equal rights. Similarly, women have been excluded from positions in the criminal justice system. Both those who supported this situation as well as those who argued for change based their arguments on sexist stereotypes. Not until recently have female offenders received attention.

1. The criminal behavior of men and women is compared. Although

crime is still a male domain, recent years have seen a rise in petty property offenses committed by women. Theories for this phenomenon are addressed including women's liberation; the feminization of poverty theory; and the increasing willingness of the judicial system to arrest and prosecute women.

2. Gender stereotypes have serious consequences for female offenders as well as female victims. Sexual assault is discussed in detail.
   a. Myths about rape continue to have a debilitating effect on successful prosecution of offenders. Victim-blaming attitudes permeate the entire proceedings.
   b. Acquaintance rape is discussed as is the treatment by the Criminal Justice system of these charges.
   c. One reason for the high rape rate in the U.S. is the prevalent belief that women are the "property" of men. A cross-cultural perspective of rape is briefly discussed.

D. THE WOMEN'S MOVEMENT AND THE GAY RIGHTS MOVEMENT: POLITICAL CONSCIOUSNESS AND SOCIAL CHANGE

The history of the women's movement and the gay rights movement is explored.

1. The abolitionist movement contributed to the rise of the women's movement. The broad- based reforms sought after by these early feminists were abandoned to gain suffrage.
2. Resurgence of the women's movement occurred during the

1960s with the founding of several feminist organizations. These groups including NOW, radical feminist groups, and socialist feminist groups are diverse in goals and orientation and have made significant gains.

3. The 1980s have shown some danger of backsliding. Since the women's movement has traditionally been one for educated, upper or middle class white women, working class and minority women have often felt that the issues pursued would have no effect on their lives. A more unified movement may emerge in the future by incorporating the needs of these women.

4. The gay rights movement has a long history in this country, however it gained momentum with the Stonewall Riots in 1969. Since then, the gay rights movement has focused on a variety of issues including the controversy of gays/lesbians in the military, AIDS research funding, and the denial of their constitutional rights.

SELF-TEST

True/False

1. The institutionalized patterns of gender differentiation in a society is known as the "sex/gender system".

   a. true
   b. false

2. The privileging of heterosexuality over homosexuality is known as homosexism.

   a. true
   b. false

3. The sociobiological perspective views masculinity and femininity as static and immutable.

   a. true
   b. false

4. Scientific evidence has proven conclusively that sexual orientation is biologically determined.

   a. true
   b. false

5. Feminist sociologists argue that gender is innately given rather than socially created.

   a. true
   b. false

6. Prehistoric females were passive, dependent childbearers.

   a. true
   b. false

7. Regardless of the society, there are always two genders which are dichotomous.

   a. true
   b. false

8. Feminists see their perspective as relevant to the concerns of both sexes.

   a. true
   b. false

9. Feminists view gender inequality as natural and even desirable under some circumstances.

   a. true
   b. false

10. Research shows that among some Asian and North American Indian societies, cross-dressed males were highly respected as the spiritual guardians of their society.

   a. true
   b. false

11. 98% of U.S. households have at least one television set.

   a. true
   b. false

12. Studies indicate a relationship between heavy television watching and sexist attitudes.

   a. true
   b. false

13. Assertions that the media engage in "symbolic annihilation" have largely proven to be unfounded.

   a. true
   b. false

14. Newspapers and news magazines depict "women's news" as unimportant, and are unlikely to feature women in stories.

   a. true
   b. false

15. Current magazines which target women are likely to feature stories on women's financial success, and the personal achievements of famous women.

   a. true
   b. false

16. Women are generally depicted less favorably than men on television with the exception that men are frequently portrayed as violent.

   a. true
   b. false

17. Studies of television programming reveal that of all racial minorities, Hispanic American men are most frequently portrayed.

a. true
b. false

18. The most common role for minorities on television are as starring roles.

a. true
b. false

19. By the time the average child in the U.S. is 18, she/he will have spent twice as much time in front of the television as she/he has in the classroom.

a. true
b. false

20. Since Title IX of the Education Amendments Act of 1972, the educational experience of men and women has been equal.

a. true
b. false

21. Currently, women make up more than 50% of college students.

a. true
b. false

22. Girls, in high school, still tend to lower their career aspirations in high school, while boys tend to raise theirs.

a. true
b. false

23. School guidance counselors and teachers often steer girls away from courses such as cosmetology and home economics because they are low paying occupations.

a. true
b. false

24. At the graduate level, female students have few available same-sex role models and mentors available to them.

a. true
b. false

25. African American women are the only female members of a minority group who have historically worked.

a. true
b. false

26. Currently, over 50% of women are in the labor force.

a. true
b. false

27. Women's participation in the labor force rose most dramatically during World War I.

a. true
b. false

28. Three of every four full-time women workers in the U.S. is a secretary.

a. true
b. false

29. Federal legislation has eliminated sex discrimination in the U.S.

a. true
b. false

30. The gap between men's and women's wages has changed very little since 1960.

a. true
b. false

31. Sexual orientation is not a protected category under the U.S constitution.

a. true
b. false

32. Recent research indicates that women are as likely to commit acts of violent crime as men.

a. true
b. false

33. Many feminists look to economic discrimination to explain the increasing number of women who are committing property crime.

a. true
b. false

34. Hate crimes committed against gays and lesbians in the U.S. have been decreasing since 1987.

a. true
b. false

35. According to FBI statistics, a woman is raped every five minutes in the U.S.

a. true
b. false

36. Women are more fearful than men because they are twice as likely to be victimized by violent crime as men.

a. true
b. false

37. Only 3% of reported rapes result in convictions of the assailant.

a. true
b. false

38. Anthropologists have established that rape is a universal phenomena. No society is "rape-free.

a. true
b. false

39. Feminists in the U.S. are a homogeneous group who are united by their membership in the National Organization for Women.

a. true
b. false

40. The Stonewall Riots of 1969 sparked the gay liberation movement.

a. true
b. false

Multiple Choice

1. __________ exists as a social category constructed on the basis of one's sex.

   a. Maleness
   b. Femaleness
   c. Gender
   d. A dichotomy

2. The difference between sex and gender is that:

   a. the former is biologically determined, whereas the latter is socially constructed
   b. the former is socially constructed, whereas the latter is biologically determined
   c. the former refers to masculinity and femininity, whereas the latter refers to a set of genetically determined traits
   d. none of the above; there is no difference between sex and gender

3. An explanation of gender through a focus on biological make-up is known as:

   a. the bio-chemical perspective
   b. the anatomical perspective
   c. the sociobiological perspective
   d. the physiological perspective

4. Which of these theorists would <u>not</u> adhere to the sociobiological perspective?

   a. Talcott Parsons
   b. Sigmund Freud
   c. Charles Darwin
   d. all of the above agreed with this perspective

5. Feminist sociologists maintain that:

   a. the world exists as an orderly social system
   b. socialization plays no role in gender acquisition
   c. gender is socially created
   d. nature is unimportant in the acquisition of gender

6. Recent studies of the connection between homosexuality and genetics have

   a. concretely linked homosexuality to chromosomal abnormalities
   b. have found that gayness is caused by one's father's genes
   c. been criticized for their methodological short-comings
   d. all of the above

7. The process through which an individual develops his/her own personality and learns the culture of one's society is known as

   a. primordialization
   b. socialization
   c. sexualization
   d. feminization and masculinization

8. Cross-cultural evidence on different societies at different times reveals:

   a. contemporary Western constructions of gender are universally accepted
   b. every known society has a division of labor by sex
   c. a gendered division of labor does not always produce gender inequality
   d. "men's work" and "women's work" is always mutually exclusive
   e. both b and c

9. Which of the following individuals is most clearly associated with cross-gendered behavior?

   a. berdache
   b. hwame
   c. alyha
   d. !kung

10. Most societies in the world are characterized by a __________ sex/gender system.

   a. matriarchal
   b. patriarchal
   c. egalitarian
   d. universal

11. A patriarchal sex/gender system:

   a. places women at the top of the social order
   b. portrays men and women as equals
   c. values men more highly than women
   d. eliminates all gender distinctions

12. Because of its critical perspective, the feminist perspective is most compatible with:

    a. functionalist theory
    b. interactionist theory
    c. sociobiological theory
    d. conflict theory

13. Studies indicate that the average household spends ____hours a day viewing T.V.

    a. two
    b. four
    c. six
    d. ten

14. The <u>reflection hypothesis</u>:

    a. claims that media content reflects dominant attitudes in society
    b. believes that women reflect the most appropriate values in society
    c. states that men and women mirror one another's actions
    d. frequently is used to explain violence between the sexes

15. The practice of ignoring, trivializing, and even condemning women is known as:

    a. systematic derogation
    b. symbolic annihilation
    c. sexist telecasting
    d. none of the above

16. Research of women in the news indicates that

    a. women are equally likely as men to be quoted in front page news stories
    b. women are equally likely as men to appear in front page photos
    c. women's news is generally portrayed as unimportant
    d. men's news is likely to be portrayed as "soft news"

17. Prime-time television:

    a. often depicts women as being educated professionals
    b. shows men as incapable of solving problems
    c. shows men using sex or charm to get their way more than women
    d. depicts women as more emotional than men

18. The research conducted by the Annenberg School of Communications found that

    a. women play an equal number of roles as men on prime-time television
    b. men outnumber women 3:1 on prime-time television
    c. women play more significant roles on cable programs than the major networks
    d. none of the above

19. Research on prime-time television reveals that:

    a. women are given more leeway in terms of their personal appearance than men are
    b. men are given more leeway in terms of their personal appearance than women are
    c. women's rights and gender equality themes are ignored
    d. there has been a vast increase in the number of Hispanic American women in central roles since the 1970's

20. On prime-time television, gays and lesbians are most likely to appear

    a. on prime-time serials
    b. as successful executives
    c. as victims of AIDS
    d. in made-for-TV movies
    e. both c and d

21. Discipline in the classroom:

    a. is dispensed more frequently to elementary school girls than boys
    b. is harsher for elementary school boys than girls
    c. has an equal effect on girls and boys in elementary school
    d. has not been studied by sociologists

22. The differential treatment boys and girls receive in elementary school results in:

    a. increased cooperative activity among boys and girls
    b. increased cooperation in same-sexed groups
    c. the reinforcement of gender stereotypes
    d. all of the above
    e. both b and c above

23. The theory that women develop lower aspirations in high school because they "fear success":

a. has been replicated by several studies
b. indicates that this fear appears to diminish as girls age
c. has been replicated with regard to boys
d. all of the above

24. Female undergraduate and graduate students:

a. often lack same-sex role models and mentors
b. are often encouraged to pursue occupations in science
c. have a decided advantage over males due to their gender
d. should not be allowed to take certain courses

25. In Bowers v. Hardwick, the Supreme Court ruled that

a. discrimination in education is unconstitutional
b. discrimination in the workforce is unconstitutional
c. discrimination against a person on the basis of sexuality is unconstitutional
d. states may criminalize homosexual acts such as sodomy even if engaged in by consenting adults in their homes

26. The gay rights movement is best characterized as

a. a unified movement without conflict
b. a diverse movement with many concerns
c. as focused primarily on AIDS
d. "dead" since the Stonewall Riots

27. In graduate education:

a. women now outnumber men in traditionally masculine fields
b. men outnumber women in many fields that at the undergraduate level were female-dominated
c. minority women outnumber white women in successfully completing degree programs
d. minorities in general now outnumber whites in successfully completing degree programs

28. Historically, the lowest paid members of the labor force have been:

a. white women
b. white men
c. minority women
d. minority men

29. After World War II, women:

a. frequently chose to keep their wartime jobs even at lower wages
b. happily returned to their homes, leaving the labor force permanently
c. would not accept low paying jobs
d. opted for domestic life with children

30. The increase in women's participation in the labor force after 1965 was a result of all of the following except:

a. decreasing fertility rates
b. expansion of the service sector
c. new divorce laws
d. governmental sponsoring of day care centers

31. Which of the following is not true of occupational sex segregation in the U.S.?

a. women are still largely segregated into "female-dominated" occupations
b. men are largely segregated in non skilled crafts, operative jobs, and labor
c. traditionally "male" jobs are more lucrative than traditionally "female" jobs
d. since 1985 we are seeing dramatic increases in the number of women into traditionally male-dominated professions

32. Which of the following is not true with regard to women in the workplace?

a. Women are often treated on the basis of their "master status"
b. Women are frequently victims of sexual harassment
c. Women have a lower commitment to their jobs and a higher commitment to the family than men
d. Women are often excluded from social networks on the basis of gender

33. Petty property offenses:

a. have decreased significantly in recent years
b. are mostly associated with men
c. have increased among women
d. do not include shoplifting

34. Which of the following is <u>not</u> evaluated by your authors as a good explanation for recent increases in women committing petty property offenses?

a. women are naturally more devious than men
b. changing shopping patterns of women
c. feminization of poverty
d. increasing willingness of the criminal justice system to prosecute women

35. With regard to female offenders, which of the following is most strongly related to sentence severity?

a. race
b. prior record
c. seriousness of crime
d. conformity to traditional norms of respectable femininity
e. both a and d

36. Studies indicate that the crime most women, in general, fear most is:

a. homicide
b. rape
c. assault and battery
d. robbery

37. To convince a court that she is a "worthy witness" a rape victim must:

a. have reported the offense promptly
b. display visible emotional trauma
c. not be in any way responsible for her victimization
d. all of the above

38. ______________ rape is the most common form of sexual assault in the U.S.

a. Marital
b. Stranger
c. Acquaintance
d. all are equally common

39. According to your text, which of the following is the best explanation for the high rate of rape in the U.S.?

a. there is an unequal power relationship between men and women
b. violence against women is condoned
c. the mentally disturbed do not receive the medical attention they so desperately need
d. all of the above
e. both a and b

40. This branch of feminism argues that the "personal is political" because male domination pervades all aspects of society.

a. Socialist feminists
b. Radical feminists
c. Liberal feminists (members of NOW)
d. all of the above

Fill in the Blanks

1. The term Symbolic annihilation applies to the media in their tendency to ignore, trivialize, and condemn women and women's issues.

2. The fear of success theory maintains that young women lower their aspirations and achievements in high school because they feel that they will be rejected socially if they are successful.

3. The privileging of heterosexuality over homosexuality is known as Heterosexualism

4. The degree to which men and women are concentrated in occupations which workers of their own sex predominate is known as occupational sex segregation.

5. Anthropological studies indicate that Rape-free societies are egalitarian, value motherhood, and see women as sources of wisdom.

Matching

1. "anatomy is destiny" Charles Darwin
2. cross-gender males A Berache
3. men dominate women and what is masculine is more highly valued than what is feminine Patriarchy
4. this perspective maintains that the media reflects the attitudes and behaviors of dominant society B Reflection Hypothesis
5. in theory, this equalized the educational experiences of men and

women
6. This event sparked the gay rights movement
7. affirmative action
8. The notion of "equal pay for work of similar value"
9. master status
10. shoplifting
11. most common form of rape is:
12. Betty Friedan
13. created in 1966 as a lobbying group for women's interests
14. they see gender inequality as intrinsic to capitalism
15. socially created definitions of masculinity and femininity
16. an attribute which takes on greater importance in the eyes of others than any other characteristic of a person
17. Talcott Parsons
18. this Supreme Court decision criminalized acts such as sodomy, even among consenting adults
19. egalitarian societies which value motherhood and women
20. sexist societies characterized by a devaluation of all that is feminine

A. berdache
B. reflection hypothesis
C. Title IX of the Educational Amendments Act
D. Edwin Schur
E. acquaintance
F. NOW
G. Charles Darwin
H. patriarchal society
I. Title VII of the Civil Rights Act
J. petty property offense
K. Socialist feminists
L. master status
M. instrumental/expressive roles
N. The Stonewall Riots
O. Bowers v. Hardwick
P. rape-free
Q. rape-prone
R. gender
S. Comparable Worth
T. The Feminine Mystique

ANSWERS TO CHAPTER 5

True/False

1.	True	21.	True
2.	False	22.	False
3.	True	23.	False
4.	False	24.	True
5.	False	25.	False
6.	False	26.	True

7.	False	27.	False
8.	True	28.	True
9.	False	29.	False
10.	True	30.	True
11.	True	31.	False
12.	True	32.	False
13.	False	33.	True
14.	True	34.	False
15.	False	35.	True
16.	True	36.	False
17.	False	37.	True
18.	False	38.	False
19.	True	39.	False
20.	False	40.	True

Multiple Choice

1.	c	21.	b
2.	a	22.	e
3.	c	23.	b
4.	d	24.	a
5.	c	25.	d
6.	c	26.	b
7.	b	27.	b
8.	e	28.	c
9.	a	29.	a
10.	b	30.	d
11.	c	31.	d
12.	d	32.	c
13.	c	33.	c
14.	a	34.	a
15.	b	35.	e
16.	c	36.	b
17.	d	37.	d
18.	b	38.	c
19.	b	39.	e
20.	e	40.	b

Fill in the Blanks

1. Symbolic annihilation
2. Fear of Success
3. Heterosexism
4. Occupational sex segregation
5. Rape-free

Matching

1. G
2. A
3. H
4. B
5. C
6. I
7. N
8. S
9. D
10. J
11. E
12. T
13. F
14. K
15. R
16. L
17. M
18. O
19. P
20. Q

CHAPTER 6

The private sphere of the "family" is not idyllic, and in this chapter some of the problems found in intimate relationships are explored. Marital power within the family is not equally distributed and this chapter examines the implications of this on the division of labor, parenting, and domestic violence. Finally, this chapter explores some of the special problems which face a growing segment of the population--single parent homes and gay/lesbian couples.

A. CONTEMPORARY FAMILIES: DIVERSITY AND CHANGE

The notion of the public/private split or the home as separate from the public sphere is a false dichotomy. Both continually interact. Although the traditional nuclear family remains the goal aspired to by the majority of Americans, statistical evidence shows that in reality isolated nuclear families represent a minority of families in the U.S today. A growing number of families are single-parent households, singles, domestic partnerships and gay and lesbian cohabiting couples. Still the ideal of the nuclear family as ideal has serious repercussions for non-nuclear families.

B. SEXUALITY AND REPRODUCTIVE FREEDOM

A brief history of contraception and abortion in the U.S. is provided.

1. Women have had the right to abortion in the U.S since 1973 with the decision of Roe v. Wade . However, the number of

abortions have been decreasing in recent years as a result of costs, threats to physicians, and the harassment of anti-abortionists.

2. Approximately 15% of U.S couples are infertile. New reproductive technologies including In-Vitro Fertilization and Surrogacy are discussed. Particular emphasis is placed on the ethical concerns generated by new technologies and the extent to which factors such as race, social class, geographic location and religious beliefs constrains one's reproductive freedom.

C. VARIETIES OF INTIMATE RELATIONSHIPS

There are a growing number of types of intimate relationships. Problems which face each type of relationship are addressed.

1. Heterosexual marriages are regulated by the marriage contract. The marriage contract, unlike any other contract, is decided and regulated by the states. Involved parties may not negotiate the terms of their agreement.

2. Marriages are power relations. Housework is an important aspect of understanding power relations in families.

   a. Housework is devalued in our society and continues to be the primary responsibility of women, even when they are employed outside the home.

   b. The notion of a "second shift" is discussed and its implications for women and the family.

3. Caregiving is an important aspect of intimate relationships. Because of women's reproductive role, they almost always have primary responsibility for child care. Our society supports and encourages this by socializing girls from early childhood to the eventual goal of motherhood.
   a. Women also have primary responsibility for caring for elderly parents.
   b. The gendered caregiving/employment model presents advantages and disadvantages for both women and men with children. The implications of an employment structure which maintains the traditional gendered division of labor in the home are discussed.

4. The number of single-parent households has been increasing, owing largely to the divorce rate and the rise in births to unmarried women.
   a. The vast majority of single-headed households are headed by women.
   b. Some observers point to the advent of no-fault divorce as the major factor in the economic hardship of these female headed households and the feminization of poverty. This issue is considered in detail.
   c. Single male-headed households are increasing in number but face few of the economic hardships of single women.

4. <u>Domestic Partnerships</u> are another popular option. Those who cohabit are less likely to stay together for the long-term and are more likely to remain childless than married couples.

5. Gay and Lesbian Partnerships represent a diverse population and often these couples face hardships in a heterosexist society. Some of the problems facing gay and lesbian couples are the failure of society to legitimate their union with official marriages, problems with receiving benefits, and restrictions and stigmatization in raising children.

D. DOMESTIC VIOLENCE

Although more is known today about domestic violence such as child abuse, spouse abuse and elder abuse, these problems continue to be widespread in our society.

1. Partner Abuse in Heterosexual Relationship. Spouse abuse is a serious problem facing the American family. However, this issue is highly contentious for both professionals and the general public.
    a. The notion of mutual battering has harmful repercussions for victims of spouse abuse. Studies indicate that women are at the greatest risk for being victimized by battering.
    b. Much research has focused on why women remain in abusive relationships. The most important reasons are financial dependence, intimidation, and personal commitment to the relationship.
    c. Lack of alternatives is one important reason some women stay. While shelters provide temporary asylum, they cannot accommodate all women who seek escape from their abusive husbands.

d. The main focus of research on battered wives should not be why these women remain, but rather what factors precipitate the abuse. Many claim that the batterer was somehow not responsible for his actions; this approach, however, fails to deal with spouse abuse as a product of the social context in which it occurs.

e. Both prevailing attitudes and the legal system have legitimized this practice through most of written history. The notion of privacy in the home seriously limits the ability of battered wives to get help and sends the message to batterers that they will not be accountable for their actions.

2. <u>Partner Abuse in Gay and Lesbian Relationships</u> is a rather new area of study and much of the research is inconclusive. However, it is clear that partner abuse does occur in gay and lesbian relationships and that the abuse can be quite severe. Also, many battered lesbians and gay men are inhibited from leaving their partners because of a lack of resources in society.

3. <u>Child abuse.</u> The conception of children as property or wild animals served to justify beatings and other forms of physical abuse throughout much of Western history. Whippings and beatings were expected, legitimized forms of discipline for all social classes in the United States well into the 19th century. Although the laws have changed, prevailing attitudes of many have not.

a. Sexual abuse is another form of abuse of which many children in our society are victims.

b. This abuse, while more common for girls, occurs with boys as well.

4. Elder Abuse. This is the term for physical or psychological mistreatment or neglect of senior citizens by an adult caretaker. Less is known about elder abuse than child or spouse abuse.

   a. It is believed that women are more likely to be victimized than men. The most common abusers are adult daughters or sons who take up the responsibility of caring for an infirm parent.

   b. More recent research uncovers more diversity in abusers as well as diversity in the factors which motivated abuse.

SELF-TEST

True/False

1. The word "family" derives from a word that means "slave or servant."

   a. true
   b. false

2. The private world of the family in no way intersects with the public world of paid employment.

   a. true
   b. false

3. The most common family form in the U.S. today is the isolated nuclear family.

   a. true
   b. false

4. The instrumental family role includes caring for children and seeing to the emotional needs of family members.

   a. true
   b. false

5. Research indicates that the majority of U.S teens have sex by the age of 19.

   a. true
   b. false

6. An estimated 10% of the U.S population self-identifies as exclusively homosexual.

   a. true
   b. false

7. By approximately 1850, abortion was outlawed in the U.S. for primarily religious reasons.

   a. true
   b. false

8. The distribution of contraceptives in the U.S. has been legal for only about 25 years during this century.

   a. true
   b. false

9. In <u>Roe v. Wade</u> the court ruled that the state must prohibit abortions within the second trimester because the fetus is "viable".

   a. true
   b. false

10. The Supreme Court's "abortion and contraception decisions" of the 1970's has made abortion and contraception equally accessible to all women.

    a. true
    b. false

11. Since the early 1990's, anti-abortion groups such as Operation Rescue have used increasingly violent means to restrict women's access to abortion clinics.

    a. true
    b. false

12. The U.S. has one of the highest rates of teenage pregnancy of Western industrialized countries.

    a. true
    b. false

13. Less than 5% of couples in the U.S. are unable to conceive or maintain a pregnancy.

    a. true
    b. false

14. There is a fear by many feminists that the practice of surrogacy portrays women as "interchangeable fetal containers".

    a. true
    b. false

15. Recent reproductive advances have raised mainly medical questions, not ethical ones.

    a. true
    b. false

16. The marriage contract is not a legally binding agreement.

a. true
b. false

17. When employed wives work full-time and also have primary responsibility for the housework, this is known as a "second shift".

a. true
b. false

18. It is only those women who do not work outside of the home who spend significantly more time on housework each week than their partners.

a. true
b. false

19. The notion of childcare and housework as "women's work" is no longer an aspect of traditional family ideology.

a. true
b. false

20. Studies indicate that egalitarian marriages are likely to become more traditional with the birth of a child.

a. true
b. false

21. Recent research indicates that men are more likely to provide care to elderly parents than women.

a. true
b. false

22. Historically in the U.S., mothers have been awarded custody of children after a divorce.

a. true
b. false

23. The majority of single-parent households are headed by men.

a. true
b. false

24. Over half of female-headed families live in poverty.

a. true
b. false

25. Studies indicate that following a divorce, women and their dependent children suffer a 73% decrease in their standard of living, whereas men enjoy a rise in their standard of living.

a. true
b. false

26. Virtually 90% of all divorced mothers are awarded child support.

a. true
b. false

27. A significantly large number of the "new poor" are couples with children.

a. true
b. false

28. Historically the black female-headed household could be characterized as "pathological."

a. true
b. false

29. The single population in the U.S consists primarily of young heterosexual men and women who have not yet married.

a. true
b. false

30. It is generally accepted that there is a single homosexual lifestyle.

a. true
b. false

31. Research indicates that couples who cohabit before marriage are more likely to divorce than those who did not cohabit first.

a. true
b. false

32. Currently there are 25 states in which gay and lesbian couples can legally marry.

a. true
b. false

33. Social scientists have studied violence in the family since the early 1800s.

a. true
b. false

34. Battery is the single major cause of injury to women in the U.S.

a. true
b. false

35. The majority of studies indicate that husbands are just as likely to be seriously victimized by battery as wives.

a. true
b. false

36. Approximately 2000-4000 women are killed each year by their partners.

a. true
b. false

37. Research indicates that gay and lesbian partnerships are generally free from violence.

a. true
b. false

38. Unwanted or unplanned children are at an especially high risk for abuse and neglect.

a. true
b. false

39. Due to recent educational programs, it is estimated that fewer than 200,000 children are abused in the U.S each year.

a. true
b. false

40. Studies indicate that almost 1 million elderly people are abused in the U.S. each year.

a. true
b. false

Multiple Choice

1. The notion that the home is separate from the public world is known by sociologists as:

   a. home/work split
   b. public/private split
   c. the dichotomy theory
   d. the separation hypothesis

2. ____ of all marriages in the U.S. end within seven years.

   a. less than 10%
   b. 25%
   c. 50%
   d. 75%

3. According to marital law, the right to decide domicile legally belongs to:

   a. the husband
   b. the wife
   c. a judge
   d. none of the above; most states no longer have domicile rights

4. The "ideal" family in the U.S.:

   a. has a single parent and dependent children
   b. has two parents who both work outside of the home and dependent children
   c. has two parents who work without children
   d. has two parents and the husband works, wife stays home, and dependent children

5. Women who work outside the home:

   a. usually have domestic help
   b. have husbands who contribute significantly more time to housework than the husbands of full-time homemakers
   c. continue to maintain primary responsibility for housework
   d. spend even more time on housework than full-time homemakers

6. Research on househusbandry indicates that:

   a. this lifestyle is growing rapidly in popularity
   b. househusbands spend more time on housework than housewives
   c. most househusbands are either temporarily out of work or work out of their home
   d. this is the only effective means to equally divide household labor between spouses

7. The rate of teenage pregnancy in the U.S. is higher than many other Western industrialized countries because:

a. U.S. youths are more sexually active
b. U.S. youths have less access to contraception
c. U.S. youths are more likely to have multiple sexual partners
d. all of the above

8. It has been argued that abortion:

a. was common among poor minority women in the 19th century
b. was never considered to be a political issue until the 1980's
c. was outlawed to allow trained physicians to take control from midwives
d. was non-existent before the 20th century

9. In Roe v. Wade, the Supreme Court ruled that:

a. a woman has an absolute right to terminate her pregnancy whenever she chooses
b. the state may not interfere with a woman's right to obtain an abortion at any time during her pregnancy
c. the state has no authority to prevent a woman from obtaining an abortion during the first trimester of her pregnancy
d. abortion is permissible only in the case of rape or incest

10. In Carey v. Population Services International, the Supreme Court:

a. overturned Roe v. Wade
b. decided to require states to provide Medicaid funding for abortions
c. struck down restrictions on the rights of minors to obtain abortions
d. extended to minors the same constitutional right to privacy as adults with regard to contraception

11. During the past 10 years the number of abortions have been declining in the U.S because:

a. fewer physicians are providing abortions
b. public opinion correctly indicates that most women will not have abortions
c. of the increasingly dangerous activities of anti-abortion groups at clinics
d. both a and c above

12. The most controversial reproductive strategy is:

   a. in vitro fertilization
   b. artificial insemination
   c. surrogacy
   d. biological fertilization

13. Couples who are unable to conceive a child or maintain a pregnancy often have difficulty utilizing some of the available options for obtaining a child because:

   a. most of these options carry serious health risks to both the parents
   b. these options are often prohibitively expensive
   c. religious, legal or ethical problems prevent them from seeking alternatives
   d. both b and c

14. Studies of childbearing have shown that:

   a. it is rare for single people to become parents
   b. men provide the most signficant amount of childcare during middle childhood
   c. men provide the most significant amount of childcare during infancy
   d. men provide equal amounts of childcare throughout a child's life

15. The addition of children to a household:

   a. increases marital satisfaction
   b. lowers marital satisfaction
   c. does not significantly disrupt the lives of the parents
   d. increases spontaneity in the marital relationship

16. Which of the following has <u>not</u> been offered by sociologists as an explanation for why women continue to play the role of primary parent?

   a. women are by nature better suited to care for children
   b. the structure of work in our society leaves women and men with few other options
   c. men provide women with subliminal cues that cause them to engage in mothering behavior
   d. women are taught to mother from an early age whereas men are not

17. In most households, women have primary responsibility for all of the following <u>except</u>:

    a. childrearing
    b. caring for elderly relatives
    c. kinkeeping
    d. they have responsibility for all of the above

18. Research indicates that elderly family members receive ______ of their care from women.

    a. 10%
    b. 25%
    c. 50%
    d. 75%

19. In comparison to father-only households, female-headed households:

    a. are fewer in number
    b. are poorer
    c. receive more help from neighbors and relatives
    d. enjoy fewer conflicts with job responsibilities

20. The most significant problem single mothers face is:

    a. society's repudiation of them
    b. finding a suitable husband
    c. economic hardship
    d. too much interference from friends and relatives

21. No-fault divorce:

    a. requires that one partner sue the other form violation of the marriage contract
    b. has done little to alleviate the conflict and stress of the divorce proceedings
    c. is available in only a handful of states
    d. has contributed substantially to increases in the number of impoverished women

22. Which of the following is true regarding child support?

    a. Minority women are more likely than white women to be awarded child support.
    b. The majority of those awarded child support receive full payments.
    c. The average child support payment has been declining in recent years.
    d. The 1984 Child Support Enforcement Act has been effective in forcing delinquent fathers to pay.

23. The poverty of many minority female-headed households is characterized best as:

a. reshuffled poverty
b. subcultural poverty
c. new poverty
d. event-driven poverty

24. Which of the following groups would not be included under the title of "singles"?

a. never-married heterosexuals
b. single parents with dependent children
c. gay men not in a committed relationship
d. all of the above are examples of singles

25. According to researchers, those involved in domestic partnerships

a. are more likely to have children than married partners
b. are likely to be together for 20 years or longer
c. are likely to be together for 2 years or less
d. are decreasing in number

26. Which of the following is true about gays/lesbians?

a. they are much more promiscuous than heterosexuals
b. most have confused sexual identities
c. being raised by a homosexual parent causes gender-identity confusion for children
d. they are not more likely than heterosexuals to molest children

27. The first country to legally recognize marriages between homosexuals was:

a. the United States
b. Sweden
c. Australia
d. Denmark

28. Research on gay and lesbian parents indicates:

a. they face fewer emotional hardships than heterosexual parents
b. that their children are no more likely to experience gender identity confusion than children of heterosexual parents
c. that they have gained increasing support from communities in raising their children
d. all of the above

29. Studies of male and female children reveal that:

a. females are significantly more likely to be sexually abused
b. females are more susceptible to neglect than males
c. neglect and abuse are not significant problems for children
d. males are more susceptible to neglect than females

30. Research on child abuse indicates:

a. that fathers are more likely than mothers to abuse children
b. that mothers are more likely than fathers to abuse children
c. that cases are over-reported by neighbors who interfere without just cause
d. that most abuse begins when the child reaches adolescence

31. Research indicates that many women do not leave battering relationships for all of the following reasons <u>except:</u>

a. they enjoy the violence
b. they think that they can change their husbands
c. economic dependence on their husbands
d. they are personally committed to the relationship
e. all of the above

32. Spouse abuse is most likely caused by:

a. a severe lack of education and low income among the abusers
b. psychological maladjustment among abusers
c. alcohol or drug dependency among abusers
d. legal and social attitudes which construct battering as acceptable in marriage

33. The phrase "rule of thumb":

a. refers to the use of a dictionary
b. derives from a law describing the stick a husband could use to beat his wife
c. was a law that allowed women to beat their children
d. was popular in the Orient in the 19th century

34. Since the 1970's:

a. there has been little change in the response of police departments to domestic violence
b. all 50 states have instituted mandatory arrest policies when the officers have probable cause to believe domestic violence has occurred
c. the majority of urban police departments have adopted mandatory arrest policies
d. it has become clear that the police can do little to deter domestic violence

35. Elder abuse:

a. has been more widely studied than spouse abuse and child abuse
b. appears to be most often perpetrated by an adult son or daughter who is caring for the parent
c. must be reported to the police in all 50 states
d. appears to be unrelated to other forms of domestic violence

36. Among the following, the group most at risk for elder abuse is:

a. men, aged 65 to 75
b. minority men
c. women, aged 75 and older
d. men, aged 90 and older

37. Which of the following contributes to the problem of elderly abuse?

a. the isolation commonly faced by many elderly
b. the lack of legislation to systematically address this problem in the U.S
c. that the elderly are devalued members of society
d. all of the above

38. Research conclusively proves that:

a. domestic violence is not a problem in gay and lesbian relationships
b. gay and lesbian partners are five times as likely to abuse each other as heterosexuals
c. battered gays and lesbians are more likely to immediately terminate a violent relationship than heterosexuals
d. like battered heterosexual women, battered gays and lesbians have difficulty leaving relationships for a variety of reasons.

39. One significant problem facing gay men who are abuse victims is

a. a lack of resources to help them leave
b. guilt for leaving if their partner has AIDS
c. lack of family support
d. all of the above

40. * The ______________ role entails leadership and decision-making responsibilities and is known as the economic provider role.

a. expressive
b. instrumental
c. fundamental
d. patriarchal

Fill in the Blanks

1. Judith Stacey calls households which expand and contract in size to fit the needs of various kin, Accordian Family.

2. In Griswold v Connecticut the Supreme Court ruled that prohibitions against married couples' use of contraception violated their rights to privacy.

3. Under NO-fault statutes, a spouse may file for divorce on the grounds of "irreconcilable differences"

4. The increasing trend of women and children living below the poverty line is known as the feminization of poverty.

5. Under common law, a husband was permitted to "correct" his wife with a stick no thinker than his thumb. This was known as Rule of thumb.

Matching

1. C the understanding that the home and public work are distinctively separate spheres
2. H mother who stays home, father who works, and dependent children
3. E Arlie Hochschild
4. A the economic provider role
5. F the nurturing role
6. D The case which decided that minors have a right to privacy, including the privacy to use contraception
7. B The case which determined that women have a constitutional right

to abortion.

8. in vitro fertilization
9. those who link the generations within the family
10. a group of people, who are not born into poverty, but are forced into it by recent life changes.
11. when poor families dissolve, and the mother and children re-form new but also poor families.
12. both husbands and wives engage in physical and psychological abuse
13. the most understudied form of domestic violence
14. the single greatest cause of injury to women in the U.S.
15. when heterosexuality is perceived as superior to homosexuality
16. families which expand and contract to respond to needs of kin
17. the first country to legalize gay and lesbian marriages
18. living together without marriage
19. no-fault divorce
20. two working parents, without children in the home

A. instrumental
B. Roe v. Wade
C. public/private split
D. Carey v. Population Services International
E. second shift
F. expressive
G. cohabitation
H. isolated nuclear family
I. event-driven poverty
J. heterosexism
K. when a couple has "irreconcilable differences"
L. battering
M. mutual battering
N. accordion families
O. elder abuse
P. Denmark
Q. kinkeepers
R. the most common family form in the U.S.
S. new poor
T. "test-tube fertilization"

ANSWERS TO CHAPTER 6

True/False

1.	True	21.	False
2.	False	22.	False
3.	False	23.	False
4.	False	24.	True
5.	True	25.	True
6.	True	26.	False
7.	False	27.	False
8.	True	28.	True

9. False
10. False
11. Trueq
12. True
13. False
14. True
15. False
16. True
17. True
18. False
19. False
20. True
29. False
30. True
31. True
32. False
33. False
34. True
35. False
36. True
37. False
38. True
39. False
40. True

Multiple Choice

1. b
2. c
3. a
4. d
5. b
6. c
7. b
8. c
9. c
10. d
11. d
12. c
13. d
14. b
15. b
16. c
17. d
18. d
19. b
20. c
21. d
22. c
23. d
24. d
25. c
26. d
27. d
28. b
29. a
30. b
31. a
32. d
33. b
34. c
35. b
36. c
37. d
38. d
39. d
40. b

Fill in the Blanks

1. Accordian family
2. Griswold v. Connecticut
3. No-fault
4. Feminization of poverty
5. Rule of Thumb

Matching

1. C
2. H
3. E
4. A

5. F
6. D
7. B
8. T
9. Q
10. S
11. I
12. M
13. O
14. L
15. J
16. N
17. P
18. G
19. K
20. R

CHAPTER 7

The problem of ageism, the use of age to define an individual's capabilities and appropriate social roles, has serious consequences for U.S. society. This chapter explores the sources of ageism and the effects of this problem on the elderly and children.

A. THE INCREASING PRECARIOUSNESS OF CHILDHOOD

The declining status of children in the U.S. and elsewhere in the world is discussed in this introductory section. It is argued that the powerlessness of children is one of the root causes of this problem. The debate about intergenerational equity is also explored.

B. THE GRAYING OF THE WORLD'S POPULATION.

The number and proportion of elderly in the U.S. has grown faster than the general population. This phenomena is occurring worldwide and much of this chapter explores the implications of this population restructuring.

C. STEREOTYPES OF AGING AND THE AGED

In U.S. society, aging is viewed as negative and, therefore, something to be concealed.

1. The historical focus of most gerontological research has been the decline of the aged. For this reason, much of the research intended to better understand aging has reinforced the negative stereotypes by essentially blaming the victim. However, many

gerontologists have begun analyses of the social system which imposes second class citizenship on the elderly. This research and the myths of aging such as all elderly are asexual and all elderly are senile, are discussed in detail.

2. Explaining ageism. There are several theories which seek to explain <u>ageism</u>.

   a. Some explanations focus on gerontophobia. It would seem that those unable to come to terms with their own mortality exhibit hostility toward the elderly whom remind them of this.

   b. Ageism is learned in the same way that other cultural values are learned, through the process of socialization. Particular focus is given to ageism in the media. Cross cultural and cross historical data indicate that in many societies, the elderly are considered valuable assets.

   c. The <u>modernization theory</u> attempts to explain the United States' transformation from a gerontophilic society to one that suffers from gerontophobia in terms of the needs of the labor force following the Industrial Revolution. Cross cultural research yields findings that question the assumptions of modernization theory.

C. GENDER, RACE, SOCIAL CLASS, AND AGING

Despite widely held conceptions of the elderly as overrepresented among the poor, the percentage of the elderly living below the poverty line has decreased in recent years. There is dramatic variation in the incomes of elderly men and women and even greater variations when race is taken into account.

1. This disparity in income among the elderly can be traced to weaknesses in the Social Security system and differential earnings which are discussed in detail.
    a. Private pension funds are offered to less than two-thirds of the labor force and compose a small amount of the aggregate income of the aged.
    b. Supplemental Security Income benefits are offered to some elderly for whom Social Security income doesn't provide an adequate amount.
    c. Bureaucratic obstacles along with strict requirements insure that many more elderly do not receive assistance from these programs.
    d. Earnings provide another from of income to the aged. However, the percentage of the work force aged 65 and over has declined steadily in recent years and continues to do so. The elimination of mandatory retirement by Congress has alleviated some of the strain on the Social Security system, but most elderly do not opt to remain in the labor force once they reach retirement age.

D. MEETING THE HOUSING AND MEDICAL NEEDS OF THE ELDERLY

Despite popular myths, fewer than 5% of all elderly people are in a nursing home at a given time.

1. A sizable percentage of the female elderly live alone, most of whom are widows. The majority of seniors in the U.S. continue to live where they resided when they were in the work force.
    a. The problems of maintaining a home for the elderly are discussed. Regular upkeep and property taxes both take a toll on the budget. This is compounded by gentrification.
    b. There are several federal or state programs which provide assistance to those who wish to maintain their homes.
    c. Another option is retirement communities and research provides inconclusive findings as to whether these age segregated environments are beneficial.
    d. Many elderly, however, now find themselves residing in naturally occurring retirement communities (NORCs), a trend which they view positively.
2. Residents of nursing homes are typically white females aged 75 and over. There are several reasons for this, including the disparity in life expectancy between men and women. In addition, minority elderly are less likely to be able to afford the costs associated with nursing homes.
3. Home care is an alternative to care in a nursing home. However, insurance coverage is limited, making it an unrealistic option for many. Home care may also be overwhelming for the caregivers who are typically middle aged women with other family members to care for and who are also employed outside the home.

E. SENIOR POWER

As the percentage of the population 65 and over increases, many social scientists have predicted an increased ability of seniors to command a certain amount of influence over policies and programs. This assumption has been criticized by those who point to the diversity of that population.

1. Studies show that, politically, the elderly most often maintain the views they held earlier and when they shift views, they do so in the same direction as their younger counterparts.
2. Data on the political participation of the elderly are presented along with an overview of their political organizations. The AARP, NCSC and the Gray Panthers are discussed as members of the Gray Lobby.

SELF-TEST

True/False

1. The United States is a society free of ageism.

   a. true
   b. false

2. Both the very young and the old are victims of "ageism."

   a. true
   b. false

3. "Geriatrics" is the study of elderly social interaction.

   a. true
   b. false

4. Research indicates that sex among the elderly is extremely rare.

   a. true
   b. false

5. Longitudinal studies test the same individuals over time.

   a. true
   b. false

6. In the U.S., the elderly have a disproportionately high suicide rate.

   a. true
   b. false

7. According to this chapter, elderly whites tend to express greater life satisfaction than elderly racial minority group members.

   a. true
   b. false

8. Gerontophobia is linked to one's inability to cope with one's own mortality.

   a. true
   b. false

9. Research indicates that age awareness is not present in most individuals until their teen-age years.

a. true
b. false

10. For the most part, senior citizens are overrepresented in the media.

a. true
b. false

11. Over 90% of television characters aged 65 and older are women.

a. true
b. false

12. In some societies industrialization brings increased respect to the elderly.

a. true
b. false

13. The majority of elderly live in poverty.

a. true
b. false

14. Cross cultural comparisons indicate that there is a greater degree of income distribution disparity among the U.S. elderly than in most other Western industrialized countries.

a. true
b. false

15. Social Security is a "progressive" form of taxation.

a. true
b. false

16. The majority of Americans are covered by private pension plans.

a. true
b. false

17. Supplemental Security Income was designed to supplement Social Security or provide for those not eligible for Social Security; however, many argue that it forces people into poverty.

a. true
b. false

18. The majority of people over 65 are not in the paid labor force.

a. true
b. false

19. Native Americans have the highest life expectancy rates among minorities.

a. true
b. false

20. Research demonstrates that older workers, have lower absenteeism, greater job stability and a more positive attitude toward work than younger workers.

a. true
b. false

21. Mandatory retirement has been abolished for almost all jobs in the U.S.

a. true
b. false

22. A higher percentage of elderly men than elderly women live alone.

a. true
b. false

23. The tendency for most elderly to "age in place" has given rise to "naturally occurring retirement communities."

a. true
b. false

24. Senior citizens are not significantly affected by property taxes.

a. true
b. false

25. In recent years, food costs have been consuming a larger percentage of the elderly's income.

a. true
b. false

26. "House-sharing" is not a popular option among senior citizens because it is considered an invasion of privacy.

a. true
b. false

27. The majority of elderly live in "retirement communities."

a. true
b. false

28. Primarily due to health reasons, over 80% of elderly men will spend some time in a nursing home before they die.

a. true
b. false

29. Nursing homes are among the most de-segregated institutions in this country.

a. true
b. false

30. The majority of nursing homes are for-profit institutions.

a. true
b. false

31. Medicare pays for virtually all of the health costs of the elderly.

a. true
b. false

32. The practice of "home care" was pioneered in the U.S.in the 1940s.

a. true
b. false

33. In 1988 Congress passed legislation to protect the rights of nursing home patients.

a. true
b. false

34. Senior citizens have been effective in lobbying for their interests because they form a homogenous group.

a. true
b. false

35. Controlling for variables such as sex, income and marital status, the elderly are more likely to vote than the young.

a. true
b. false

36. The largest organized interest group in the country is the American Association of Retired People.

a. true
b. false

37. Advances in telecommunications are likely to make it more difficult for elderly people to engage in political activities.

a. true
b. false

38. The refusal of older people to characterize themselves as "elderly" is known as <u>age consciousness.</u>

a. true
b. false

39. An examination of the Index of Social Health of Children and Youth indicates that the overall status of U.S. children is declining.

a. true
b. false

40. The U.S. was the first country to sign the Convention on the Rights of the Child created by the United Nations General Assembly.

a. true
b. false

<u>Multiple Choice</u>

1. "Ageism" is defined as:

a. the upgrading of the social class composition in a neighborhood
b. an unreasonable fear of aging
c. using age to define one's abilities
d. a sharp decline in memory and intelligence

2. _______________ countries are witnessing the most dramatic growth in the number of elderly.

a. Third World
b. Developing
c. Western Industrialized
d. No (all countries are experiencing a decline in the number of elderly)

3. The world will be composed largely of older societies in the next century primarily because of:

   a. declines in fertility
   b. extended life expectancy rates
   c. maturation of post-WWII generations
   d. all of the above

4. Which of the following is <u>not</u> a common stereotype of older people?

   a. they are "set in their ways"
   b. they move and think more slowly
   c. they become asexual
   d. they become increasingly liberal

5. The field of gerontology:

   a. has historically ignored or discouraged sexual activity among the elderly
   b. historically contributed to much faulty knowledge about aging
   c. originally focused on the physical decline of the aged
   d. all of the above

6. Studies of elderly sexuality indicate:

   a. that the elderly are basically asexual
   b. one's pattern of sexuality in later life parallels earlier sexual patterns
   c. post-menopausal women frequently lose all of their sex drive
   d. most elderly people find their partners physically "repulsive"

7. Research of the intellectual ability of the aged indicates:

   a. intellectual ability drastically declines with age
   b. memory loss occurs in over 80% of the elderly population
   c. the majority of elderly are senile
   d. intellectual ability remains relatively stable over time

8. Recent research indicates that senility occurs in:

   a. over 90% of those over the age of 80
   b. roughly half of elderly men
   c. roughly three-quarters of elderly minority women
   d. in approximately 5% of those over the age of 65

9. Which of the following stereotypes of the elderly is true?

   a. the majority are senile
   b. the majority are asexual
   c. the majority are isolated and lonely
   d. none of the above

10. In commercials that use elderly males:

    a. health aides and laxatives are typically advertised
    b. older generations are portrayed as independent and capable
    c. women are seen as the dominant spouse
    d. the setting is always a nursing home

11. Studies indicate that ageism is:

    a. an attitude with which we are born
    b. learned through the process of socialization
    c. is present in every society
    d. historically a problem in the U.S.

12. In colonial times, Americans had:

    a. gerontophobia
    b. modernized
    c. gerontophilia
    d. none of the above

13. A common critique of modernization theory is:

    a. a devaluation of the elderly began to take place in the U.S. prior to industrialization
    b. not all pre-industrial societies devalue the elderly
    c. some industrialized societies value the elderly
    d. all of the above

14. Which of the following societies does/did not hold the elderly in high esteem?

    a. Samoans of Polynesia
    b. Coast Salish Indians
    c. Colonial Americans
    d. all of the above respect/respected the elderly

15. Since the 1960s:

    a. the poverty rate of the elderly has dramatically increased
    b. the poverty rate of the elderly has dramatically decreased
    c. the poverty rate of the elderly has stayed the same
    d. poverty for the elderly has been virtually eliminated.

16. The poverty rate for the elderly has been reduced because of all of the following reasons <u>except:</u>

    a. Social Security benefits have been increasing
    b. The elderly are more likely than young people to own their own home and this is an asset
    c. An improved index for poverty has for the first time accurately counted the number of aged poor
    d. More elderly have private pension plans than those in the past

17. Which of the following is most likely to live in poverty?

    a. a single elderly white man
    b. a married elderly white couple
    c. a single elderly African American woman
    d. a single elderly Asian American woman

18. The authors of this text argue that a policy of ________ ________ for Social Security would be less discriminatory towards elderly women.

    a. regressive taxation
    b. progressive taxation
    c. earnings sharing
    d. adequate replacement rate

19. Programs like subsidized housing, food stamps, Medicare and Medicaid:

    a. are benefits that are available to all elderly
    b. are known as in-kind income
    c. are available only to citizens under 65
    d. have succeeded in lifting America out of poverty

20. The Social Security's "retirement test":

    a. is given to everyone over 65 to test their capacity for future employment
    b. has been ruled as discriminatory by the Supreme Court
    c. allows retirees to earn a certain income and still collect full benefits
    d. is exploitative of elderly people

21. Workers who are ushered in and out of the labor force as they are needed:

    a. are referred to as a "reserve army of labor:"
    b. are often employed by elderly employers
    c. compose the majority of the AFL/CIO
    d. often command the top seats in small businesses

22. Studies indicate that currently ____ of the elderly live in nursing homes.

a. 75%
b. 50%
c. 20%
d. less than 5%

23. Studies of the relationship between the official crime rates and fear of crime among elderly widows show:

a. even when crime rates are high, widows usually claim to feel safe
b. elderly widows feel apprehension even when crime rates are low
c. high crime rates are directly correlated with levels of fear among elderly widows
d. elderly widows are usually committing crime and thus, have less fear

24. The process of upgrading the social class composition and housing stock within a neighborhood is:

a. progressive taxation
b. gentrophilia
c. the Graying of America
d. gentrification

25. Which of the following refers to the communities which develop as a result of the elderly's tendency to "age in place?"

a. "property tax circuit breaker"
b. HELP
c. RAMS
d. NORCs

26. The trend to convert apartments into condominiums:

a. displaces those elderly who cannot afford the increased monthly fees
b. has generally worked to the benefit of older Americans
c. was started by retired workers to make a quick profit
d. has backfired against developers because of the lack of interest

27. Most elderly in the U.S. prefer:

a. to live in retirement communities
b. to live with relatives
c. to age in place
d. to live in nursing homes

28. The "typical" nursing home resident is all of the following <u>except</u>:

a. 75 years old or older
b. female
c. married
d. white

29. Studies of for-profit nursing homes have found that they are likely to:

a. discriminate against members of racial minorities
b. charge more money per day than Medicaid covers
c. force the elderly to engage in a policy of "spending down"
d. all of the above

30. The person most likely to care for an impaired elder is:

a. a spouse
b. a nursing home aide
c. a female spouse or daughter
d. a male spouse or son

31. Studies of the political orientation of the aged indicate that:

a. the aged are a homogenous group
b. the aged are politically conservative
c. the aged do not undergo "political socialization"
d. with age, people tend to become more moderate in their beliefs

32. In 1988, Congress passed a law to protect:

a. the rights of nursing home patients
b. the right of the AARP to stage demonstrations
c. the rights of home-care providers
d. none of the above

33. Research on the political participation of the elderly reveals:

a. the elderly are less likely to vote than young people with similar characteristics
b. the elderly are as likely to participate in political activities as young people with similar characteristics
c. the elderly are less likely to join political organizations than young people
d. none of the above

34. Which of the following is the largest senior citizens' group?

a. the Gray Panthers
b. the National Council of Senior Citizens
c. the American Association of Retired Persons
d. the Elderly Womens' Coalition

35. A common criticism of the gray lobby is:

a. they will have little power in the next 20 years because fewer people are joining the political interest groups
b. they were not interested in lobbying for the Age Discrimination in Employment Act of 1986
c. they do not show enough concern for the most disadvantaged elderly, elderly women
d. all of the above

36. In the U.S. children have always been treated as:

a. "innocent, cuddly creatures"
b. "wild animals who often required severe punishment"
c. "miniature adults"
d. none of the above

37. According to UNICEF:

a. less than 10% of children world-wide are malnourished
b. 40,000 children die each day world-wide
c. two thirds of the children dying world-wide die from easily remedied diseases
d. both b and c above

38. Which of the following is <u>not</u> a problem facing children in the U.S.?

a. homelessness
b. child abuse
c. poverty
d. all of the above are problems

39. Common arguments regarding children and poverty include all of the following <u>except:</u>

a. there are so many child advocacy organizations that they cannot unite to find a single solution to poverty
b. intergenerational inequity contributes to poverty
c. budget cuts during the Reagan/Bush administration contributed to poverty
d. children are powerless because they do not vote

40. The U.S. faces less severe social security problems than other industrialized nations because:

- a. U.S. citizens save more money during their youth
- b. other countries do not have private pension plans
- c. the demographic characteristics affecting the U.S. are more pronounced in other countries
- d. none of the above

Fill in the Blanks

1. Gerontophobia ______ is defined as an unreasonable fear of aging which manifests itself in hatred toward old people.

2. The theory which argues that as a society industrializes, the status of the elderly will progressively decline, is known as MODERNIZATION THEORY.

3. Most people 65 and older continue to inhabit the dwellings they did while they were working and this phenomena is known as AGING IN PLACE.

4. The federally financed health insurance program for the elderly is MEDICARE.

5. Groups such as the AARP, Gray Panthers, and NCSC compose the GREY LOBBY.

Matching

1. Using age to define one's ability
2. The demographic term for the fact that the number of elderly in the U.S. has grown quicker than the general population
3. the medical care of the aged
4. the study of the cultural factors of aging
5. a rejection of the status of "aged"
6. an unreasonable fear of aging
7. a society in which the elderly are respected
8. workers ushered into and out of the labor force to meet the needs of business
9. when the elderly still live in the place they did while they were working
10. upgrading the housing and social class composition within a given neighborhood
11. institutions run "for profit"

12. the popular alternative to caring for the impaired elderly in an institution
13. temporary supervision of an ill or disabled person provided in order to relieve the primary caregiver
14. the degree to which the elderly constitute a political force
15. it is estimated that between 8,000 and 10,000 new members join every working day
16. the group which is most likely to live in poverty in the U.S
17. characterizing the elderly as "youthful" or "middle aged"
18. international bill of rights for children
19. the use of age to define one's individual capabilities
20. residential areas which naturally have at least 50% of the population over 60 years old

A. geriatrics
B. reserve army of labor
C. ageism
D. gentrification
E. proprietary
F. Graying of America
G. avoidance psychosis
H. gentrophilic
I. home care
J. age consciousness
K. respite care
L. children
M. Convention of the Rights of the Child
N. senior power
O. ageism
P. age in place
Q. NORC
R. Social Gerontology
S. Gerentophobia
T. AARP

ANSWERS TO CHAPTER 7

True/False

1. False
2. True
3. False
4. False
5. True

21. True
22. False
23. True
24. False
25. True

CHAPTER 8

The chapter begins with a discussion of the PEON program which is fictional but not far removed from the educational system in the U.S. This chapter examines some of the ways in which schools perpetuate inequality through testing practices, tracking, and the hidden curriculum. There is also a focus on the quality of U.S. education and some of the problems which plague this institution.

A. EDUCATIONAL EXPENSES

With the rising cost of education, more and more students rely on financial aid or loans to finance their education.

1. Stringent requirements disqualify many students with genuine need from receiving most forms of financial assistance, including the Guaranteed Student Loan.
    a. Because of the increasing expense, enrollments of racial minorities in post-secondary education has declined and continues to do so.
2. Although private elementary and secondary schools rely largely on tuition and other fees, public elementary and secondary schools depend on local property tax revenue. This results in a disparity in the quality of education offered between inner city districts and wealthy suburban neighborhoods.
    a. The impact of the shift from federal to state funds on inner city schools has been severe.
    b. Since racial minorities are disproportionately

represented among the inner city poor, they are perhaps the most severely affected.

B. RACIAL SEGREGATION AND DESEGREGATION IN THE SCHOOLS

Although officially illegal, segregation persists due in large part to the disproportionate racial composition of certain school districts. The most controversial solution to this has been busing. Another alternative to this problem is magnet schools which although expensive, seem to increase academic achievement.

C. SCHOOLS AS SORTING MACHINES

Inequality in the educational system is addressed in detail.

1. Some of the underlying assumptions of tracking are presented. The consequences of tracking contradict these good intentions. Studies have found that students do not profit from being in a homogenous group and a self fulfilling prophecy develops with students labeled average and slow learners. Critics claim that students are not tracked based on academic abilities, but on other arbitrary factors.
2. Based on the false assumption that one's I.Q. was inherited, the I.Q. test was used as justification for forced sterilization of those determined to be "mentally unfit." Critics of the I.Q. test continue to question this test's ability to accurately measure intelligence and the presence of a cultural bias in the test. Both I.Q. tests and tracking legitimate and perpetuate inequality in our society.
3. In addition to the <u>formal</u> curriculum, schools have a <u>hidden</u>

curriculum as well. References to the contributions of racial minorities and women in U.S. history are conspicuous by their absence. This sends a message to students that minorities and women have not contributed in a significant way.

4. Upon examination of the distribution of employment in education, we find a glaring lack of racial minorities and the vast majority of women are concentrated at the elementary school level. This leaves females and minorities with few role models to emulate.

D. CONFRONTING THE ISSUE OF "QUALITY EDUCATION"

Abundant evidence illustrates the inadequacy of the U.S. school system to educate its students. Among this evidence is the fact that 1/3 of the adult population is semi-literate. Critics disagree as to the causes of this. However, a few common themes emerge.

1. The low prestige and low salaries accompanying teaching positions in elementary and secondary schools insure that the most qualified individuals look elsewhere for employment.
2. Critics maintain that educators spend too much time studying educational methods and theories and too little time on subject matter. Evidence supports claims that these courses do not provide prospective teachers with adequate or appropriate training.
3. Parents and colleagues do not provide a supportive environment for teachers, causing a growing dissatisfaction among teachers.
4. Practices by which teachers are trained and selected in other industrialized nations are discussed. Increasing teacher salaries and requiring a greater amount of time spent studying the

subject rather than teaching methods are obvious alternatives to our present system.

5. Students in the U.S, on average, spend less time on homework than their peers in other industrialized nations. Although television is one distraction that may contribute to this, more likely explanations deal with the lack of order in the class room and the reduction of requirements to induce increased flexibility in the curriculum. However, all 50 states have enacted policies whose goals are to upgrade the educational system.

SELF-TEST

True/False

1. PEON is a factual educational program designed to track students based on race or ethnicity.

   a. true
   b. false

2. In the 1994-95 school year, the tuition to some of the most prestigious colleges and universities exceeded $25,000.

   a. true
   b. false

3. In recent years more students are relying on loans than grants to finance their educations.

   a. true
   b. false

4. The college enrollment of African American men has increased significantly in recent years.

   a. true
   b. false

5. In the past 15 years, we have seen a decrease in the number of foreign nationals with temporary visas who are PhD recipients in the U.S.

   a. true
   b. false

6. The parental choice programs have been criticized for increasing educational inequities.

   a. true
   b. false

7. Under the Reagan administration, the federal government significantly increased federal funding of public education.

   a. true
   b. false

8. The block grant plan has been instrumental in shifting funding so that the majority of disadvantaged children receive remedial services.

   a. true
   b. false

9. Education specialist, Ernest Boyer, warns that urban U.S. schools may shortly become an "educational Third World".

   a. true
   b. false

10. By 1995, it is expected that one-third of U.S. public school students will be minorities.

    a. true
    b. false

11. Since the 1954 Brown v. Board of Education decision, schools in the U.S. have been largely desegregated.

    a. true
    b. false

12. The majority of Hispanic American and African American students are enrolled in schools which have over a 50% minority enrollment.

    a. true
    b. false

13. Under most busing desegregation plans, white children are usually bussed longer distances and for a greater number of years than minority students.

    a. true
    b. false

14. African American children are disproportionately concentrated in a few school districts.

    a. true
    b. false

15. Magnet schools appear to be effective in promoting desegregation.

    a. true
    b. false

16. African Americans have never argued against the desegregation of schools.

    a. true
    b. false

17. Tracking in U.S. schools does not generally begin until secondary school.

    a. true
    b. false

18. Tracking generally benefits "slow learners."

    a. true
    b. false

19. Different tracks are exposed to similar learning opportunities that over time have a cumulative impact on academic performance.

    a. true
    b. false

20. Within the U.S. educational system it is not uncommon for children to switch from one track to another.

    a. true
    b. false

21. After compulsory sterilization laws were deemed constitutional, over 20,000 eugenic sterilizations were performed in the U.S.

    a. true
    b. false

22. The creator of the IQ test believed that his test could accurately determine levels of intelligence and allow the government to "gradually raise the overall intelligence of society".

    a. true
    b. false

23. Most research indicates that IQ tests are good measures of a child's ability to perform in school.

    a. true
    b. false

24. What is considered "general knowledge" varies cross-culturally and from one generation to the next.

    a. true
    b. false

25. Studies indicate that the recent rise in overall IQ scores may be the result of formerly disadvantaged groups adopting a white middle-class culture.

    a. true
    b. false

26. Research on Head Start programs indicate they are "a waste of time and taxpayers' money."

    a. true
    b. false

27. The hidden curriculum is as significant in conveying knowledge to students as the formal curriculum

    a. true
    b. false

28. Racial minorities and women are overrepresented in elementary school text books.

    a. true
    b. false

29. The majority of Minneapolis-St. Paul elementary school students believe that only can become president of the U.S.

    a. true
    b. false

30. The majority of elementary school principles in the U.S. are women.

    a. true
    b. false

31. Approximately 30 million people in the U.S. are illiterate.

    a. true
    b. false

32. Many universities now require students to take at least one course on racial and cultural diversity.

    a. true
    b. false

33. In the last ten years, SAT scores have been consistently rising.

    a. true
    b. false

34. Compared to their Chinese counterparts, U.S. students are deficient in math achievement.

    a. true
    b. false

35. A variety of measures indicate that more than 1/3 of all adults in the U.S. are semi-literate.

    a. true
    b. false

36. New PhD's are opting for careers in education due to recent salary increases.

    a. true
    b. false

37. The Center for Disease Control found that over 1/3 of high school boys carry weapons to school.

    a. true
    b. false

38. Unlike the U.S., "teacher abuse" is not a problem in Japanese society.

    a. true
    b. false

39. Inequality is preserved through segregated schools, tracking and the hidden curriculum.

    a. true
    b. false

40. Compared to Japanese students, U.S. students do significantly more hours of homework each night.

a. true
b. false

Multiple Choice

1. Which of the following is true about the U.S. educational system?

a. it fosters equality for all regardless of race, ethnicity or sex
b. it perpetuates inequality through testing and tracking policies
c. most schools have instituted the PEON program with marked success
d. it is the most inexpensive program for students in the world

2. Between 1980 and 1994, basic student charges:

a. rose at a rate close to the consumer price index
b. decreased 14% after adjustment for inflation
c. remained consistent with the rise of inflation
d. rose 150% at U.S. colleges and universities

3. Research indicates that most students fund their college education with:

a. Pell grants
b. federal financial aide
c. loans
d. scholarships

4. The Clinton administration has been criticized for:

a. significantly increasing the number of students who are eligible for federally-guaranteed student loans
b. implementing policies which allow only the "most deserving" students to receive aid
c. increasing the number of poor and minority students who are eligible for financial aid
d. increased federal spending on education while decreasing the number of students eligible for financial aide

5. Racial minorities:

   a. are expected to have a decline in enrollment at colleges and universities during the next decade
   b. are expected to have an increase in enrollment at colleges and universities over the next decade
   c. are affected positively by changes in the GSL programs
   d. rarely utilize available financial aid programs to attend college

6. Due to the overall decline in financial aid and the rise in costs of education, it is expected that all of the following will occur <u>except</u>:

   a. the number of college graduates who plan to attend graduate school will decline
   b. the number of minority students will decline
   c. the number of middle class students will increase
   d. the number of upper income students will increase

7. The financing of public elementary and secondary schools through local property taxes results in:

   a. greater control of the school by the community
   b. increased vulnerability of the school to citizen's tax revolts
   c. differential spending on education between districts
   d. all of the above

8. Studies indicate that per pupil spending in low income areas:

   a. is relatively equivalent to per pupil spending in middle and higher income areas
   b. is as much as nine times less than per pupil spending in wealthy areas
   c. is less than in wealthy areas because parents spend a lesser proportion of their income on education
   d. none of the above

9. Research on the parental choice program indicates:

   a. that all students are likely to benefit from this model
   b. that the quality of all schools within a district improve under this model
   c. that children of poorly educated or non-English speaking parents are likely to remain in inferior schools
   d. that children of poorly educated parents are most likely to be switched to the best schools

10. A block grant plan is:

a. a federally funded educational program
b. a state funded educational program
c. a community based educational program
d. an eastern European educational program

11. Which of the following is true about federal funding of elementary and secondary education in the U.S.?

a. funding has increased consistently over the past 20 years
b. the U.S. spends a larger percentage of its gross domestic product on education than any other developed program
c. most federal money goes to remedial programs for disadvantaged students
d. most federal money goes to upper income neighborhoods to fund <u>Head Start</u>

12. <u>Brown v. Board of Education</u>:

a. ruled that racially segregated schools are unconstitutional
b. upheld a previous decision of separate but equal
c. led to a quick desegregation of U.S.schools
d. ended negative racial attitudes in U.S. schools

13. Research on the effects of busing has found that:

a. minority educational achievement improves
b. improved race relations among students
c. great parental opposition to these programs
d. all of the above as the studies show mixed results

14. Studies indicate that desegregation has a positive impact on education under all of the following circumstances <u>except:</u>

a. when it occurs early in the child's education before racial prejudices are ingrained
b. when teachers have inner-city and multi-ethnic teaching experience
c. when extracurricular activities such as sports in which one group of students naturally is superior, are eliminated
d. when minority teachers are available to act as role models for minority students

15. Magnet schools are appealing because they are based on:

a. careerism
b. voluntarism
c. technical aptitude
d. socialism

16. Some minority group members have recently been arguing against school desegregation because:

    a. they feel that money spent on busing could be better spent in traditionally underfinanced minority schools
    b. minority schools better meet the unique needs of minority students
    c. minority students do not need to be exposed to diversity
    d. both a and b

17. ___________ is the process whereby students are sorted on the basis of their supposed intellectual abilities into different classes.

    a. magneting
    b. tracking
    c. blocking
    d. "open classroom"

18. The practice of tracking is supposed to benefit:

    a. "slower" students
    b. intellectually gifted students
    c. teachers
    d. all of the above

19. Studies of tracking indicate that:

    a. the self-esteem of slower students is raised by being in homogenous groups
    b. tracking benefits the "brighter" students
    c. all students seem to benefit from being in homogeneous groups
    d. a self-fulfilling prophecy often occurs

20. A study by Rosenthal and Jacobsen found that:

    a. most schools do not engage in tracking
    b. although schools engage in tracking, this practice has little effect on students' performances
    c. students randomly identified as "gifted" improved twice as much as other students
    d. students identified as "slow" improved twice as much as other students because they received extra help

21. The majority of students in the U.S. are assigned to:

    a. above average tracks
    b. average tracks
    c. below average tracks
    d. both b and c

22. When asked what the most important things a student should learn during the school year are, teachers of low-trackers were most likely to respond with all of the following <u>except:</u>

a. independence
b. how to cope with frustration
c. how to keep clean
d. to begin and end each day with a smile

23. Some researchers argue that children in lower tracks are taught:

a. knowledge which is highly valued in this society such as balancing one's checkbook
b. how to fit in and the lowest level of the social and economic hierarchy
c. how to quickly ascend the social and economic ladder
d. how to be successful in leadership roles

24. Forced sterilization of those determined by IQ tests to be mentally unfit was advocated by:

a. Nobel Prize winners
b. desegregationists
c. eugenicists
d. early feminists

25. In _________________________ the Supreme Court deemed compulsory sterilization laws constitutional.

a. Roe v. Wade
b. Brown v. Board of Education
c. Buck v. Bell
d. none of the above; the courts never supported forced sterilization

26. ____________________ is a modern advocator of eugenics.

a. Alfred Binet
b. Carrie Buck
c. Robert Graham
d. Herbert Spencer

27. Most educators agree that IQ tests are good predictors of:

a. innate intelligence
b. a child's future financial success
c. a child's ability to perform in school
d. a person's ability to reproduce "smart" children

28. The IQ test has been criticized as being:

a. culturally specific
b. culturally diverse
c. too cross-cultural
d. an inaccurate measure of levels of culture

29. The IQ test was designed to:

a. determine who should be forcibly sterilized
b. determine who was eligible to go to college
c. measure innate intelligence in humans
d. identify mildly retarded and learning disabled children

30. The value preferences children are taught in school is the:

a. hidden curriculum
b. formal curriculum
c. valued curriculum
d. none of the above; values are taught in the home

31. The traditional curriculum:

a. largely ignores the contributions of racial minorities
b. focuses on women primarily as wives to important men
c. frequently portrays Native Americans as "savages"
d. all of the above

32. Which person is the most unlikely to be found as a full professor in an elite university?

a. a white man
b. a white woman
c. a black man
d. a black woman

33. Elementary school textbooks have been accused of being:

a. racist
b. sexist
c. heterosexist
d. all of the above

34. Which of the following is <u>not</u> a program used to overcome educational inequality?

a. the establishment of women's studies programs
b. cooperative learning
c. the hidden curriculum
d. a multicultural curriculum

35. The National Commission on Excellence in Education's 1983 report:

   a. showed Americans were generally better educated than expected
   b. revealed the severity of problems in U.S. education
   c. claimed that U.S. schools were improving the quality of education
   d. found that American students ranked highly in international comparison

36. Compared to students from other nations, U.S students have particular difficulty with:

   a. math
   b. geography
   c. history
   d. all of the above

37. The average salary for elementary and secondary school teachers:

   a. is significantly lower than starting salaries in other professions that require a college education
   b. has risen to levels comparable with other professions, resulting in an increase in education majors
   c. contributes to making teaching an attractive profession
   d. reflects the U.S. commitment to quality education

38. Teacher training programs are criticized for overemphasizing:

   a. fieldwork
   b. academics
   c. mathematics
   d. pedagogy

39. Comparative studies of the U.S and Japanese educational systems reveal:

   a. U.S students spend more time on homework than Japanese
   b. Japanese teachers spend more time on academics than U.S teachers
   c. a decreasing number of Japanese teachers are experiencing "teacher abuse"
   d. none of the above

40. A study by the Centers for Disease Control indicates that:

   a. very few high school students carry weapons to school
   b. almost 1/3 of high school boys carry weapons to school
   c. assaults on high school teachers by students are almost non-existent
   d. the number of high school students assaulting teachers has declined in the past 10 years

Fill in the Blanks

1. The decision of ________________________________ ruled racially segregated schools unconstitutional.

2. When children adjust their performance and self-image to meet adult expectations, this is know as a ________________________.

3. IQ tests appear to measure one's familiarity with _____ and_____ _________norms.

4. The average high school student in the U.S. spends approximately ___hours a week on reading and studying.

5. The ________________________ approach to education included the contributions, experiences and perspectives of diverse racial and ethnic groups in the population.

Matching

1. primary federal grant program for undergraduate students
2. the most popular federal loan program
3. federally funded program to improve the reading and math levels of minority and poor students
4. schools in minority neighborhoods which offer certain areas of specialization in their curriculum
5. placing students of similar intellectual abilities into specific classes
6. this movement advocated forced sterilization of those who tested "mentally unfit" by IQ tests
7. this decision ruled forced sterilization laws constitutional
8. this decision ruled "separate but equal" policy of school segregation as unconstitutional
9. Robert Graham
10. Alfred Binet
11. sperm bank for Nobel Prize winners
12. value preferences taught in school
13. reading, writing and arithmetic
14. an African American woman who wrote the second book to be published by a woman in America
15. the first physician to successfully perform a heart operation in the U.S.
16. the inability to read or write
17. when one's reading and writing skills do not allow one to cope with the responsibilities of everyday life
18. the learning of teaching techniques and educational theory
19. the number of hours elementary school students in U.S spend on average studying and reading each week
20. the educational approach which includes learning of the contributions of racial/ethnic minorities and women

A. Head Start program
B. tracking
C. modern advocator of eugenics
D. created the IQ test
E. semiliterate
F. Pell grant
G. Eugenics
H. hidden curriculum
I. illiterate
J. pedagogy
K. Stafford Student Loan Program or GSL
L. Brown v. Board of Education
M. Repository of Germinal Choice
N. formal curriculum
O. Phillis Wheatley
P. multiculturalism
Q. 4.5
R. Daniel Hale Williams
S. Buck v. Bell
T. magnet schools

ANSWERS TO CHAPTER 8

True/False

1. False
2. True
3. True
4. False
5. False
6. True
7. False
8. False
9. True
10. True
11. False
12. True
13. False
14. True
15. True
16. False
17. False
18. False
19. False
20. False
21. True
22. False
23. True
24. True
25. True
26. False
27. True
28. True
29. True
30. False
31. True
32. True
33. False
34. True
35. True
36. False
37. True
38. False
39. True
40. False

Multiple Choice

1. b
2. d
3. c
4. b
5. a
6. c
7. d
8. b
9. c
10. d
11. c
12. a
13. d
14. c
15. b
16. d
17. b
18. d
19. d
20. c
21. d
22. a
23. b
24. c
25. c
26. c
27. c
28. a
29. d
30. a
31. d
32. d
33. d
34. c
35. d
36. b
37. a
38. d
39. b
40. b

Fill in the Blanks

1. Brown v. Board of Education
2. Self-fulfilling prophecy
3. White and middle class
4. 5.6
5. Multicultural

Matching

1. E
2. K
3. A
4. T
5. B
6. G
7. S
8. L
9. C
10. D
11. M
12. H
13. N
14. O
15. R

16. I
17. E
18. J
19. Q
20. P

CHAPTER 9

Health is influenced by far more than individual eating habits and lifestyles. The definition of health is a social product influenced by historical, cultural, and political circumstances. Heath and illness are social conditions as well as physical states and this chapter examines the structural arrangements which affect the collective health of society. The health status of people in the U.S. is also compared with that found in other countries.

A. THE SOCIAL NATURE OF MEDICAL CONCEPTS

In the past definitions of health have been problematic because traditionally health was defined as the absence of illness. Two theoretical models of health and illness are emphasized here.

1. The model of health that remains predominant today is the functional model. According to this model, a healthy person is analogous to a machine in perfect working order. Illness is seen as a temporary disruption of the functioning of the person. A system of care operating under this model is oriented toward curative medicine as opposed to preventative medicine. For the most part health care in the United States emphasizes cure over prevention.
2. Critics of this model find the experiential model more attractive. According to this model, health is a complete state of physical, mental, and social well-being. Government has the responsibility to provide the level of care that will maintain this standard for all its citizens.

B. HEALTH IN THE UNITED STATES

By looking at various indicators of health we may learn the status of health in the United States.

1. Within the United States, mortality rates in most areas have declined sharply since 1950 with the notable exception of homicide, cancer, and liver disease. The infant mortality rate has also declined, while life expectancy has increased. However, when these figures are compared to infant mortality and life expectancy in other equally or less industrialized nations, the United States fares less favorably. In fact some areas of the United States are comparable to those in the least economically advantaged countries with regard to infant mortality rates. This concretely demonstrates that some Americans enjoy significantly better health than others, and this becomes even more obvious when examining sex, social class, and race.
2. The longevity gap between the sexes persists and continues to widen. Conformity to traditional masculinity appears to explain the higher mortality rates of men for heart disease, stroke, cancer, accidental death, homicide, and suicide.
3. One disease which women are at greater risk of contracting is the AIDS virus. In particular, minority women and their children are at great risk of contracting this disease. Myths and facts about AIDS are discussed in detail.
4. Social class has been shown to negatively influence self assessments of health and curtail activities due to the chronic health problems of the poor.

5. Race is responsible for a greater disparity in the mortality rate than sex. The infant morality rate of non-whites is substantially higher than that of whites. Homicide rates for African Americans, especially young African American men, are far higher than those for whites.

C. HEALTH CARE IN THE UNITED STATES

Instead of an efficient centralized system of health care, the United States currently experiences a decentralized effort that can best be described as a mosaic. In order to focus on specific problems, various aspects of health care are examined.

1. Reports have warned of an impending doctor glut that would drive up costs of medical care and encourage unnecessary treatment. Additional problems have already surfaced.
    a. Overspecialization has resulted in a chronic shortage of primary care physicians.
    b. Maldistribution compounds the unavailability of primary care physicians. Rural areas and urban neighborhoods populated by low-income minorities suffer most.
2. The mounting costs of medical care, especially hospital care, can be explained in part by advanced medical technology and by the corporate ownership of hospitals. This is known as the medical-industrial complex.
   The "for-profit" orientation of corporate owned hospitals, while driving costs up, has led to the in-

creased availability of other facilities, such as free standing emergency centers. For-profit corporate hospitals, however, can have tragic effects for would be patients whom are turned away for their inability to pay.

D. INSURING OUR NATION'S HEALTH

When they were enacted, the goal of programs such as Medicare and Medicaid was to provide equal access to medical treatment for U.S. citizens, regardless of their income. The success of these programs has been very limited.

1. Medicare, a federal health insurance plan for those 65 and over in reality covers less than half of the expenses of its beneficiaries. Specific reasons for this are highlighted and various problems resulting from this are discussed.
2. Medicaid was designed to cover the medical expenses of those unable to pay, young or old. Despite the increased medical services available to the poor, critics contend that this care is of lower quality than that given to those who can afford costly medical care. Medicaid beneficiaries are often refused treatment and many poor are not granted eligibility.
3. A large percentage of those living in the U.S. are uninsured. Many hospitals refuse to treat uninsured persons, and those that do lose billions on un-reimbursed care. HMO plans reduce employers medical costs, but this solution has done little to help the

uninsured.

4. Strategies for solving the medical insurance crisis are discussed, including the possibility of socialized medicine. il.

E. A HEALTHY MIND

Another important aspect of health that cannot be overlooked is mental health.

1. Negative stereotypes pervade definitions of mental illness. The medicalization of deviance has led to the categorization of many conditions within the psychiatric field. Critics of traditional definitions claim that mental illness is a social construction. Sex and race may influence diagnosis. Also, conceptions of mental illness vary over time and cross-culturally.
2. Several estimates of the number of treated and untreated persons suffering from different mental disorders are discussed. Variations in rates of specific disorders by sex and race are examined. The extent of drug abuse and alcohol abuse is outlined briefly.
3. The Rosenhan experiments are discussed as well as the implications of his findings for the identification and treatment of mental illness.
4. The move toward deinstitutionalization is summarized along with the resulting problems. Funds are lacking to help the deinstitutionalized adjust. Reinstitutionalization is one option, but not one preferred by many critics of the mental health system.
5. Other problems of the mental health care system, including sexual abuse of patients by their therapists, are discussed.

SELF-TEST

True/False

1. Currently the United States is experiencing a "fitness craze" in which Americans are spending more than 12 billion dollars a year on sports clothing.

   a. true
   b. false

2. Health is generally defined in positive terms as a state of well being.

   a. true
   b. false

3. Definitions of health and illness are frequently manipulated for political purposes.

   a. true
   b. false

4. Health and illness are physical states as well as social conditions.

   a. true
   b. false

5. Preventative medicine focuses on those who are already ill and has been the primary model of healthcare in the U.S.

   a. true
   b. false

6. In the U.S. society, health care is similar to other businesses with its focus on profit-making.

   a. true
   b. false

7. The majority of U.S citizens perceive health care as a fundamental right to be protected by the government.

   a. true
   b. false

8. The infant mortality rate in some U.S. cities is higher than that of some of the least economically developed countries.

   a. true
   b. false

9. The U.S. is the wealthiest country in the world in terms of per capital GNP.

   a. true
   b. false

10. Social class does not play a role in health service availability

   a. true
   b. false

11. In 1991, women could be expected to live 7 years longer than men.

   a. true
   b. false

12. Currently women are more likely to have "type A" personalities than men.

   a. true
   b. false

13. Men are more likely than women to be successful in their attempts to kill themselves.

   a. true
   b. false

14. It is expected that by the year 2000, 40 million people worldwide will have been infected with AIDS.

   a. true
   b. false

15. The most likely way of becoming infected with the AIDS virus is through transfusions of contaminated blood.

   a. true
   b. false

16. Women are more likely than men to contract the AIDS virus through heterosexual intercourse.

   a. true
   b. false

17. Currently there is no vaccination against the AIDS virus and no cure.

    a. true
    b. false

18. The higher black infant mortality rate can be explained by genetic factors.

    a. true
    b. false

19. The life expectancy of African Americans is six years longer than that of whites.

    a. true
    b. false

20. White females have the highest rate of criminal victimization in the U.S.

    a. true
    b. false

21. Research indicates that poor children are twice as likely as affluent children to have physical and mental disabilities.

    a. true
    b. false

22. The overwhelming majority of physicians practice general or family medicine.

    a. true
    b. false

23. Physicians tend to be over-concentrated in rural areas in the U.S because of better costs of living.

    a. true
    b. false

24. Because of government programs, foreign born physicians represent a significant percentage of those practicing medicine in medically underserved rural areas in the U.S.

    a. true
    b. false

25. The growth in health care expenditures can be largely explained by the increasing cost of prescription drugs.

    a. true
    b. false

26. The case of Bakke v. the Regents of the University of California established that a "quota system" for minority admissions is unconstitutional.

    a. true
    b. false

27. Studies have shown sexism, racism and negative attitudes toward the poor within the medical profession.

    a. true
    b. false

28. The fact that the U.S. population spends more money per capita on health care explains why the U.S. population has a longer life expectancy than those in Japan, Great Britain, and Canada.

    a. true
    b. false

29. "Docs-in-a-box" (free-standing emergency and routine care centers) have been criticized as expensive, time consuming and less pleasant than traditional hospitals.

    a. true
    b. false

30. Medicare currently pays less than half of the health care expenses of the elderly.

    a. true
    b. false

31. There is little evidence that low-income people have been significantly aided by Medicaid.

    a. true
    b. false

32. Less than 50% of those living below the poverty line receive Medicaid.

    a. true
    b. false

33. Less than 10% of the U.S. population is currently uninsured.

a. true
b. false

34. The U.S is the only Western industrialized nation which does not insure medical care for its population.

a. true
b. false

35. Mentally disturbed individuals are generally unpredictable and potentially violent.

a. true
b. false

36. Definitions of what constitutes "insanity" varies cross-culturally.

a. true
b. false

37. In the U.S. stereotypical masculine behavior is assumed by many clinicians to be the ideal standard of mental health.

a. true
b. false

38. Cross-addiction (simultaneous addiction to alcohol and drugs) affects men more often than women.

a. true
b. false

39. <u>O'Connor v. Donaldson</u> established that individuals who are a danger neither to themselves nor to others cannot be confined against their will without being treated.

a. true
b. false

40. Incidents of therapists sexually abusing their patients in the U.S are extremely rare.

a. true
b. false

Multiple Choice

1. One's health is influenced by each of the following except:

   a. diet
   b. exercise
   c. social class
   d. all of the above

2. Definitions of health:

   a. vary cross-culturally
   b. are static and non-varying
   c. pertain only to physiological characteristics
   d. are not influenced by political ideology

3. Under the Reagan administration:

   a. most cancers were attributed to industrial causes
   b. most cancers were attributed to non-industrial causes
   c. the causes of cancer were seen as the same as during the Carter administration
   d. cancer was attributed to liberalized medicine

4. The predominant model of health in medicine and the social sciences is:

   a. the conflict model
   b. the symbolic-interactionist model
   c. the functional model
   d. the Weberian model

5. The functional perspective is oriented towards __________ medicine.

   a. preventative
   b. curative
   c. herbal
   d. non-intervention

6. In the U.S., health care is seen as:

   a. the government's responsibility
   b. the "society's" responsibility
   c. the individual's responsibility
   d. none of the above

7. The perspective that health is "a complete state of physical, mental, and social well-being" is known as:

   a. the functional model
   b. the conflict model
   c. the intrapersonal model
   d. the experiential model

8. All of the following causes of death have decreased since 1950 <u>except</u>:

   a. polio
   b. whooping cough
   c. cancer
   d. heart disease

9. Which of the following has <u>not</u> been decreasing since 1950?

   a. infant mortality rate
   b. mortality rate
   c. life expectancy
   d. morbidity rate

10. Which of the following countries ranks lowest with respect to infant mortality rates among industrialized nations?

    a. Japan
    b. Spain
    c. Unties States
    d. Great Britain

11. Which U.S. city has the highest infant mortality rate?

    a. San Diego
    b. Houston
    c. Detroit
    d. Washington D.C.

12. Which of the following is <u>not</u> thought to be responsible for the longevity gap between men and women?

    a. genetic factors
    b. hormonal differences
    c. women's higher susceptibility to heart disease and stroke
    d. conformity to traditional gendered behavior

13. The fastest growing group of smokers in the U.S. is:

a. men over the age of 40
b. women over the age of 40
c. men under the age of 23
d. women under the age of 23

14. As a result of behavioral differences, men are more likely than women to die from:

a. cancer
b. chronic liver disease
c. accidental death
d. homicide
e. all of the above

15. In the United States:

a. the governement has been quick to respond to the threat of AIDS
b. the government has been promoting widespread condom use to prevent AIDS since 1985
c. has funded needle exchange programs since 1990
d. the government has been slow to provide funding for AIDS research

16. The fastest growing category of AIDS cases is:

a. IV drug users
b. bisexual men
c. homosexual men
d. heterosexuals

17. Among women, which racial/ethnic group is most likely to contract HIV?

a. Hispanic
b. Native American
c. Caucasian
d. African American
e. all of the above

18. All of the following is true regarding children and AIDS <u>except:</u>

a. AIDS is the ninth leading cause of death among children aged 1-4 today
b. most pediatric cases of AIDS are among white children
c. children of AIDS infected mothers have a significant chance of being infected at birth
d. none of the above

19. Misinformation about AIDS has led to which of the following tragic consequences?

    a. street violence against gays
    b. AIDS patients losing their jobs
    c. infected children denied school entry
    d. all of the above

20. With regard to life expectancy:

    a. sex is a more important factor than race
    b. race is a more important factor than sex
    c. there are no racial disparities
    d. African Americans have a longer life expectancy than whites

21. Non-white infants are more likely than white infants:

    a. to be vaccinated against serious diseases
    b. to have higher birth-weights
    c. to have higher infant mortality rates
    d. to receive pre-natal care

22. The leading cause of death for African American men aged 15-24 is:

    a. homicide
    b. cancer
    c. sickle-cell anemia
    d. car accidents

23. Regarding the connection between social class and health, research indicates that:

    a. there is no correlation between good health and social class
    b. the poor are more likely than the upper class to rate their health as "good"
    c. the poor are more likely than those with higher incomes to have their activities limited from chronic illnesses
    d. poor children actually receive better routine primary care than those in the middle class

24. Doctors are more likely to become specialists because:

    a. the median net income is greater for specialists than general practitioners
    b. specialists work fewer hours a week than general practitioners
    c. specialists work more regular hours than general practitioners
    d. all of the above

25. The medically underserved are found primarily:

   a. in rural areas of the U.S.
   b. in poor areas of large cities
   c. outside of the U.S.
   d. both a and b above

26. The expansion of corporate medicine has:

   a. created virtually a socialist system of medicine
   b. increased the autonomy of individual physicians
   c. focused attention on cost-cutting mechanisms and increased profits
   d. all of the above

27. Which of the following exacerbated the problem of low minority attendance to medical schools?

   a. the <u>Bakke v. the Regents of University of California</u> decision
   b. government funding cuts to financial aid programs
   c. curtailing the National Health Service Corps
   d. all of the above

28. Health care expenditures have increased in the U.S. due to all of the following factors <u>except</u>:

   a. the increased number of elderly in the U.S. seeking medical attention
   b. the increasing number of hospitals owned by the federal government
   c. increasing price of drugs
   d. the proliferation of advanced medical technology

29. The expansion of corporate-owned hospital chains:

   a. has led to poor management of hospitals by medical staffs
   b. has shifted priorities away from productivity and cost efficiency
   c. has benefited the investors, pharmaceutical firms and equipment suppliers of hospitals
   d. has benefited those who are insured by the government

30. The implementation of Medicare:

   a. has provided equal access to medical care for all in the U.S.
   b. gave comprehensive coverage to all elderly people
   c. led many people to eliminate their "medigap" policies
   d. has encouraged many physicians to provide excessive and expensive care

31. Which of the following is <u>not</u> true with regard to Medicaid:

   a. Many doctors refuse to treat Medicaid patients because of its low reimbursement level
   b. Medicaid reimbursements are on average 79% of what it costs to treat a hospitalized Medicaid patient
   c. Eligibility for Medicaid is decided solely by the federal government
   d. Many elderly poor receive Medicare and Medicaid

32. Which group of people is likely to be uninsured?

   a. those who work for small businesses
   b. children
   c. single mothers living under the poverty line with dependent children
   d. all of the above
   e. both a and b

33. Cost shifts and related measures in Medicare and Medicaid:

   a. have fallen most heavily on the elderly and the poor
   b. result in senior citizens and the poor being less cost conscious
   c. are likely to reduce health care costs
   d. have worked to reduce the financial strain of the poor

34. The American Medical Association:

   a. has always campaigned against national health insurance, claiming it is socialistic
   b. shaped its opinions in light of public opinion polls on the subject of national health insurance
   c. once advocated the establishment of national health insurance for equitable distribution of medical resources in the U.S.
   d. has never publicly come out with a unified position on the issue of national health insurance

35. The "medicalization of deviance":

   a. gave power to religious figures to determine who was mentally ill
   b. recognized psychoanalysts as experts in the treatment of mental illness
   c. placed the "problems of living" in the domain of psychiatric medicine
   d. occurred in 1970

36. Which of the following disorders is found almost exclusively within Western cultures?

a. agoraphobia
b. koro
c. anorexia nervosa
d. all of the above
e. both a and c above

37. The de-medicalization of homosexuality in the Diagnostic and Statistical Manual for Mental Disorders:

a. occurred in 1900
b. occurred in 1950
c. occurred in 1980
d. has not yet occurred despite serious lobbying efforts by gay/lesbian activists

38. The group with the highest rate of depression is:

a. married men
b. minority and poor women who head households
c. never-married women
d. elderly women in rural areas

39. The Rosenhan studies indicate that:

a. most patients in psychiatric hospitals are schizophrenic
b. most patients in psychiatric hospitals are women
c. experts cannot distinguish the sane from the insane
d. pseudo-patients were quickly diagnosed as sane and removed from psychiatric hospitals

40. All of the following are problems facing the mental health care system except:

a. high incidence of sexual abuse of patients by their therapists
b. treatment by therapists which focuses on the "adjustment" of patients to the existing status quo
c. deinstitutionalization of those who are still mentally ill
d. the establishment of egalitarian relationships between therapists and their patients

Fill in the Blanks

1. The ____________________________ is based on an understanding of the human body as analogous to a machine.

2. There is considerable evidence that the problem facing the American health care system is not too many doctors but ________________ and ________________________.

3. The name for the federal health insurance plan for those aged 65 and older is ________________.

4. The ______________________ decision resulted in a massive wave of deinstitutionalization.

5. Erving Goffman coined the phrase ____________________ to describe the dehumanizing effects of institutionalization.

MATCHING

1. functionalist perspective
2. this type of medicine focuses on those who are already ill
3. this type of medicine focuses on the conditions which preclude the outbreak of illness in the first place
4. the number of deaths in proportion to the given population
5. the number of deaths of children under 1 year of age per 1000 live births
6. the average number of years of life remaining for an individual at a given age
7. a person who exhibits coronary prone behavior
8. the "killer" disease which has infected 10 million people globally
9. too many doctors who are highly specialized
10. too many doctors who are concentrated in particular geographic areas
11. the fastest growing segment of the population at risk for contracting the HIV virus
12. the federal health insurance plan for those 65 and older
13. the federal and state health insurance plan for the poor
14. prepaid health plans
15. a publicly-financed and publicly-controlled program to ensure equitable access to health care
16. his studies indicated that it is difficult for those in the mental health profession to discern "normality from abnormality"
17. disorders which include depression and anxiety
18. a disorder characterized by social withdrawal, delusions, fears, and hallucinations
19. having a simultaneous addiction to both alcohol and drugs
20. the decision which ruled that individuals who are not a danger to themselves or others cannot be confined against their will without treatment

A. AIDS
B. overspecialization
C. Rosenhan
D. Talcott Parsons
E. Type A personality
F. curative
G. maldistribution
H. mortality rate
I. life expectancy
J. health maintenance organizations (HMO)
K. heterosexuals
L. schizophrenia
M. preventative
N. affective disorders
O. Medicare
P. cross-addiction
Q. Socialized medicine
R. infant mortality rate
S. Medicaid
T. O'Connor v. Donaldson

ANSWERS TO CHAPTER 9

True/False

1. True
2. False
3. True
4. True
5. False
6. True
7. True
8. True
9. False
10. False
11. True
12. False
13. True
14. True
15. False
16. True
17. True
18. False
19. True
20. False
21. True
22. False
23. False
24. True
25. True
26. True
27. True
28. False
29. False
30. True
31. False
32. True
33. False
34. True
35. False
36. True
37. True
38. False
39. True
40. False

Multiple Choice

1. d
2. a
3. b
21. c
22. a
23. c

4.	c	24.	d
5.	b	25.	d
6.	c	26.	c
7.	d	27.	d
8.	c	28.	b
9.	c	29.	c
10.	a	30.	d
11.	d	31.	c
12.	c	32.	d
13.	d	33.	c
14.	e	34.	a
15.	d	35.	a
16.	d	36.	e
17.	d	37.	c
18.	b	38.	b
19.	d	39.	c
20.	b	40.	d

Fill in the Blanks

1. Functional model of health
2. Overspecialization, maldistribution
3. Medicare
4. O'Connor v. Donaldson
5. A total institution

Matching

1. D
2. F
3. M
4. H
5. R
6. I
7. E
8. A
9. B
10. G
11. K
12. O
13. S
14. J
15. Q
16. C
17. N
18. L
19. P
20. T

CHAPTER 10

The problem of crime is a concern for most United States citizens. Despite the overall fear of crime, the probability of becoming a victim is actually declining for most of the U.S. population. This chapter focuses on theoretical explanations of crime; including biological, social and radical theories; as well as on how crime is measured. Violent crime is addressed as well as corporate and political crime. Finally, the complex relationship between drug use and criminality is discussed.

A. WHY DO PEOPLE COMMIT CRIMES?

A historical perspective is taken on the issue of criminality. Many of the early theories relied on biological explanations of criminality. More recent theories focus on the social causes of crime.

1. The earliest theories of crime focused on individuals and their biological make-up to explain crime.
    a. Cesare Lombroso believed that certain people were "born criminals" and that atavism caused crime
    b. William Sheldon focused on somatotyping and argued that mesomorphs were the most likely population to commit crimes
    c. Henry Goddard used IQ tests to argue for a link between feeblemindedness and criminality. His research had serious implications for the issue of eugenic sterilization.
2. Later theories focused on sociological theories of crime.
    a. Shaw and McKay were concerned with social disorganization and

crime in urban areas.

b. Cloward and Ohlin coined the phrase "differential opportunity" to explain that not everyone n society has equal access to societal resources and this is related to crime.

c. A connection has also been drawn between broken-homes and delinquency. This theory is evaluated.

3. Radical criminology focuses on the issues of power and social class to explain criminality. In contrast to other theories, radical criminology argues for fundamental changes in society's social structure.

B. THE CRIME PROBLEM

Crime is broadly defined by the federal government as any act for which there is a formally prescribed punishment.

1. One primary source of national crime statistics is the Uniform Crime Reports. One important shortcoming of this data source is that it only reflects the number of crimes known to police. Other criticisms of this source of data on crime are presented.

2. An alternative source of information on crime in the United States is the National Crime Survey, a federal victimization study. According to their findings, less than a third of violent personal crimes or household crimes are reported to authorities.

C. VIOLENCE

Clearly, the United States is the most violent of all Western democracies. Of particularly significant concern today is the widespread usage of guns. Equally important is the growing number of young people who are not only victimized by violent crime, but are also the perpetrators.

D. THE OTHER SIDE OF CRIME

This section focuses on the serious nature and costs of white-collar crime, better known today as economic and political crime.

1. The introduction of <u>white collar crime</u> refocused discussion of crime from lower-class urban centers to crime in the corporate sector. Although much white collar crime lies in a gray area, these offenses are unquestionably unethical.
   a. Offenses committed by employees against employers are workplace crimes.
   b. A more diverse body of offenses, occupational crime, occurs when an individual takes advantage of his/her position to secure something of value. Members of the medical and financial community are among those who engage in this type of crime.
   c. Organizational crime differs from occupational crime in that the offenders are top ranking decision-makers for corporations who, for profit or survival, engage in illegal business activities. Price-fixing, product dumping and a variety of other activities constitute organizational crime and the ramifications are felt by not only U.S workers and consumers, but by citizens of other countries as well.
   d. Organized crime has consistently held a prominent position in

U.S. law enforcement. This type of crime draws extensive profits, is diversified, and operates within a highly structured organization, much as corporations do.

2. White-collar crime is generally not perceived by the public to be as serious as violent crime. However, the costs of these types of crime are indeed, great.

E. DRUGS AND CRIME

An increasing focus has been placed on drug use in the U.S and the connection between drugs and crime.

1. Factors which have contributed to the nation's renewed concern with drug abuse are analyzed. The effects of alcohol and drug use on behavior is discussed.
2. Gender is an important factor when one considers the relationship between drugs and crime. Particular attention is paid to women who engage in prostitution to either earn money for drugs or directly exchange sex for drugs.
3. For the past decade there has been a growing concern with the drug "crack." The spread of this drug and the implications are discussed.
4. The U.S. government has taken steps to curb drug distribution in the U.S. These steps, and the efforts of foreign governments are evaluated.

SELF-TEST

True/False

1. According to the Crime Clock, one violent crime occurs every 22 seconds.

   a. true
   b. false

2. The probability of becoming a victim of a violent act increases every day for Americans.

   a. true
   b. false

3. A person over the age of 65 is the most likely to be a victim of violent crime.

   a. true
   b. false

4. Cesare Lombroso argued that criminals were biological degenerates.

   a. true
   b. false

5. William Sheldon argued that the tendancy to become criminal is hereditary.

   a. true
   b. false

6. Henry Goddard's work focused mainly on somatotyping.

   a. true
   b. false

7. As a result largely of Goddard's work, more than 30 states passed laws permitting forced sterilization of those deemed to be "feebleminded."

   a. true
   b. false

8. In their work, Shaw and McKay argued that criminality was caused by social disorganization.

   a. true
   b. false

9. Cloward and Ohlin located crime as a problem primarily of the middle and upper class who had the "differential opportunities" to commit most crimes.

 a. true
 b. false

10. Currently one of the mostly widely known explanations for crime is the "broken home hypothesis."

 a. true
 b. false

11. Radical criminologists advocate fundamental changes in society's social structure to eliminate crime.

 a. true
 b. false

12. Radical criminologists are the least likely to focus on social class as a variable in explaining criminality.

 a. true
 b. false

13. Over 90% of the total U.S. population is represented in the <u>Uniform Crime Report</u>.

 a. true
 b. false

14. The <u>Uniform Crime Reports</u> cover many serious offenses including corporate and organized crime.

 a. true
 b. false

15. The <u>Crime Index Offenses</u> includes only violent crimes.

 a. true
 b. false

16. White collar crime receives relatively low scores on "severity" when rated by the public.

 a. true
 b. false

17. The <u>Uniformed Crime Report</u> presents only those "crimes known to the police" and thus represents about 1/3 of all crimes committed.

    a. true
    b. false

18. Property offenses are committed much less frequently than violent crimes.

    a. true
    b. false

19. The reporting of crime is a value-neutral process.

    a. true
    b. false

20. Property crimes are the most likely to be "cleared" by the police.

    a. true
    b. false

21. The UCR has been criticized for over-emphasizing hidden crime.

    a. true
    b. false

22. The <u>National Crime Survey</u> is the major federal study of victimization.

    a. true
    b. false

23. From <u>National Crime Surveys</u>, we know that only 7% of crimes result in a charge being filed against a suspect.

    a. true
    b. false

24. The <u>National Crime Surveys</u> indicate that most people report incidents of violent crime.

    a. true
    b. false

25. Rape is the type of violent crime for which the offender is most likely to be prosecuted and sentenced to prison.

    a. true
    b. false

26. The majority of Americans believe that there is a connection between crime rates and violence on television.

    a. true
    b. false

27. Compared to other Western democracies, the U.S. is the least violent society.

    a. true
    b. false

28. According to UCR statistics, the homicide rate is increasing in the U.S. each year.

    a. true
    b. false

29. There are more than 200 million privately owned firearms in the U.S.

    a. true
    b. false

30. Edwin Sutherland coined the phrase "white collar crime".

    a. true
    b. false

31. Politicians have immunity from being charged with committing occupational crimes.

    a. true
    b. false

32. Generally, the white-collar criminal is an unsuccessful and poorly respected member of society.

    a. true
    b. false

33. Annually, over 100,000 U.S workers die from occupational health hazards.

    a. true
    b. false

34. The cost of white-collar crime far exceeds that of street crime.

    a. true
    b. false

35. The U.S. public's view of drugs has been one of intolerance for the past 50 years.

a. true
b. false

36. Research indicates that the majority of juvenile crime is drug related.

a. true
b. false

37. Women appear to be more prone to crack addiction than to other forms of drug addiction.

a. true
b. false

38. It is estimated that at least 100 billion dollars a year is spent in the U.S. on illegal drugs.

a. true
b. false

39. Research indicates that the usage of crack cocaine has been rising exponentially in the 1990's.

a. true
b. false

40. Peru is one of the few countries that has made an effort to curtail drug production.

a. true
b. false

Multiple Choice

1. Research indicates that one's likelihood of being victimized by violent crime is influenced by:

a. race
b. age
c. gender
d. all of the above

2. Which of the following theorists did not explain crime with biological theories?

   a. Cesare Lombroso
   b. Ernest Hooton
   c. William Sheldon
   d. Lloyd Ohlin

3. Which theorist argued that crime was caused by people being "born criminal" or atavism?

   a. Lloyd Ohlin
   b. Shaw and McKay
   c. Cesare Lombroso
   d. William Sheldon

4. According to William Sheldon, the person most likely to become criminal is a:

   a. mesomorph
   b. ectomorph
   c. endomorph
   d. eclectomorph

5. As a result of Goddard's tests on feeblemindedness

   a. it was conclusively proven that low IQ scores make one likely to commit crimes
   b. it was conclusively proven that high IQ scores make one likely to commit crimes
   c. thirty states passed laws permitting the forced sterilization of those diagnosed as feebleminded
   d. all 50 states eliminated sterilization laws

6. Who focused on social disorganization to explain criminality?

   a. William Sheldon
   b. Shaw and McKay
   c. Cloward and Ohlin
   d. Eleanor Glueck

7. Cloward and Ohlin explained criminality with the concept of

   a. atavism
   b. concentric zones
   c. somatotyping
   d. differential opportunity

8. Official statistics indicate that:

   a. most delinquents come from broken homes
   b. family structure is strongly related to seriousness of delinquency
   c. officials respond more harshly to children in broken homes than in intact homes
   d. both a and c above

9. Radical criminologists are likely to focus on:

   a. social class
   b. body types
   c. family structure
   d. IQ rates

10. Which of the following is <u>not</u> a major source of national crime statistics?

   a. <u>Uniformed Crime Reports</u>
   b. <u>Crime Index Offenses Survey</u>
   c. <u>National Crime Survey</u>
   d. all of the above are major sources of national crime statistics

11. Statistics in the <u>Uniform Crime Report</u>:

   a. are provided voluntarily
   b. are reported by police departments on a mandatory basis
   c. represent only 25% of the U.S. population
   d. cover only 5 major categories of crime

12. Which of the following is <u>not</u> a Crime Index Offense?

   a. forcible rape
   b. murder
   c. aggravated assault
   d. motor vehicle theft
   e. all of the above are covered

13. Which of the following is a common criticism of the <u>Uniformed Crime Report</u>?

   a. it places too much emphasis on "hidden crime"
   b. it places too much emphasis on index crimes
   c. it does not accurately represent all reported crime
   d. all of the above

14. The Uniformed Crime Report indicates that between 1982 and 1992, the population whose rate of victimization increased most significantly was

a. elderly white women
b. young white men
c. young African-American men
d. elderly African-American women

15. The National Crime Survey indicates that:

a. virtually all crime is reported to the police
b. less than 1/3 of crime is reported to the police
c. violent crime is more likely to be reported than property crime
d. victims of violent crime are likely to report and be ignored by the police

16. National Crime Survey data indicates that the most likely crime to be reported to the police is:

a. violent personal crime
b. property crime
c. arson
d. all crimes are vastly under-reported

17. With regard to National Crime Survey finding on rape:

a. 90% of victims report the crime to the police
b. all those who are convicted go to prison
c. 90% of those who are charged are prosecuted
d. over 90% of rapists go unpunished

18. According to UCR statistics:

a. murders most often occur between members of different races
b. most murders are intra-racial
c. the homicide rate in the U.S. is small in comparison to other industrialized countries
d. all of the above

19. Which of the following is most likely to be a victim of homicide?

a. a white woman
b. an African American woman
c. a white man
d. an African American man

20. High rates of violence in the U.S have been correlated with:

a. high rates of gun ownership
b. lax federal control of licensing
c. increases in violent crime by youths
d. all of the above

21. According to violent crime data:

a. people under the age of 18 are committing violent crime at growing rates
b. people under the age of 18 are the most likely to be victimized by violent crime
c. gang violence has decreased markedly since 1985
d. all of the above
e. both a and b above

22. Which of the following is <u>not</u> a category of business-related crime?

a. workplace crime
b. organized crime
c. occupational crime
d. organizational crime

23. Occupational crime:

a. is committed only by white collar workers
b. is treated more casually by the judicial system than violent crime
c. is perceived by the public as quite "serious"
d. is not likely to be found in the medical or financial fields

24. This form of crime involves "decisionmakers" of corporations who engage in illegal activities.

a. corporate crime
b. organizational crime
c. occupational crime
d. workplace crime

25. All of the following are victims of corporate crime <u>except:</u>

a. workers in the corporation
b. the general public
c. populations of other countries
d. all of the above are victims of corporate crime

26. Which of the following is <u>not</u> an example of corporate crime?

    a. product dumping
    b. dumping of hazardous waste products
    c. price fixing
    d. all of the above are examples of corporate crime

27. The U.S. government has been accused of engaging in which type of criminal activity?

    a. overthrowing foreign "unfriendly" governments
    b. condoning the exportation of unsafe products to Third World countries
    c. invading the privacy of U.S. citizens in the honor of "national security"
    d. all of the above

28. White collar criminals are:

    a. likely to receive harsher sentences than those who commit crimes against property
    b. likely to receive "community service" as punishment
    c. more likely to be tried in court than violent criminals
    d. likely to receive harsher fines than other criminals

29. Organized crime has been implicated in which of the following illegal activities?

    a. loansharking
    b. drug distribution
    c. gambling
    d. all of the above

30. The estimated percentage of high school seniors in the U.S. who have used cocaine is:

    a. 2-5%
    b. 10-13%
    c. 20-30%
    d. over 50%

31. Crack, a purified form of cocaine:

    a. causes addiction quicker than heroine
    b. is primarily distributed on the streets, by gangs
    c. produces erratic behavior
    d. all of the above

32. Compared to men who use drugs, women are more likely:

    a. to commit violent crime
    b. to be victims of violent crime
    c. to exchange sex for drugs
    d. to experience less stigmatization

33. The most widely used drug in the U.S is:

    a. cocaine
    b. crack
    c. heroine
    d. marijuana

34. Research indicates:

    a. that drugs/alcohol and crime are 100% correlated
    b. that alcohol use decreases the likelihood of one committing violent crime
    c. that marijuana usage decreases the likelihood of one committing violent crime
    d. that there is a complex relationship between drug/alcohol use and crime

35. Drug trafficking is now controlled mainly by

    a. street gangs
    b. organized crime
    c. the U.S government
    d. foreign governments

36. Which administration has spent the most money to curtail drug distribution in the U.S?

    a. Carter
    b. Reagan
    c. Bush
    d. Clinton

37. Which of the following countries has made the most progress in curtailing drug production and distribution?

    a. Columbia
    b. Haiti
    c. Peru
    d. Nicaragua

38. Which type of offense are juveniles more likely to commit than older age groups?

 a. violent crimes
 b. white-collar crimes
 c. serious property crimes
 d. all of the above

39. The Crime Act by Congress in 1991:

 a. mandated military involvement in the war on drugs
 b. eliminated aid to foreign countries who do not try to stem drug production and distribution
 c. established a mandatory death sentence for drug-related murders in federal cases
 d. none of the above

40. The population most at risk for using crack currently is:

 a. the poor
 b. women
 c. children
 d. all of the above

Fill in the Blanks

1. Cloward and Ohlin argued that crime is caused by ______________ ____________________.

2. _________________________________ are likely to advocate changes in our social structure to reduce crime

3. The ________________________________ is based on officially reported crime statistics.

4. ____________________ coined the phrase white-collar crime

5. ______________ crimes involve the willful attempt of an individual to take advantage of their professional position to secure something of value.

Matching

1. focused on atavism to explain crime
2. focused on somatotyping to explain crime
3. the type of person most likely to commit a crime
4. connected IQ levels and crime
5. the 8 offenses on which the FBI collects data on for the UCR
6. this terms refers to the number of individuals who are arrested and charged with an offense and turned over to the court for prosecution

SELF-TEST

True/False

1. Every year there are thousands of new laws enacted to govern behavior in the U.S.

   a. true
   b. false

2. Karl Marx developed the consensual model of law creation.

   a. true
   b. false

3. Karl Marx argued that crimes violated a society's "collective conscious."

   a. true
   b. false

4. The vast majority of laws are subject to identical influences and evolve in a similar setting.

   a. true
   b. false

5. A pluralist would argue that laws don't necessarily reflect a consensus.

   a. true
   b. false

6. An elitist would argue that laws are created by powerful groups in society.

   a. true
   b. false

7. Crisis theory maintains that laws sometimes reflect consensus and sometimes reflect the interests of the elite.

   a. true
   b. false

8. The Sherman Anti-trust Act was the first federal effort to control commerce in the U.S.

   a. true
   b. false

9. The Sherman Anti-trust Act effectively curtailed corporate monopolization.

   a. true
   b. false

10. Prior to 1914, the use of opiates in the U.S. was legal.

   a. true
   b. false

11. Research indicates that in states which require mandatory sentences with jail time for those found guilty of DUI, the vast majority of offenders are not jailed.

   a. true
   b. false

12. Surveys indicate that the majority of Americans have "great confidence" in our justice system.

   a. true
   b. false

13. The vast majority (over 85%) of police officers have baccalaureate degrees.

   a. true
   b. false

14. Over 80% of police operations have fewer than twenty-five officers.

   a. true
   b. false

15. Compared to rural police departments, urban departments adhere to a more "legalistic" form of law enforcement.

   a. true
   b. false

16. In his research, James Wilson found that the majority of police officers spend most of their time on law enforcement.

   a. true
   b. false

17. For most of the 20th century, policing in the U.S has best been identified as "community policing."

   a. true
   b. false

18. "Strategic policing" strategies challenge the criminal directly.

    a. true
    b. false

19. Community policing identifies community members as partners in solving crimes.

    a. true
    b. false

20. Community policing models have been widely embraced by most police departments in the U.S.

    a. true
    b. false

21. Studies indicate that African Americans are arrested more frequently for minor offenses and treated with greater force than whites.

    a. true
    b. false

22. The Wickersham Commission of the 1920's documented the widespread nature of police brutality.

    a. true
    b. false

23. Research on policing practices indicate that most officers use excessive force on a regular basis.

    a. true
    b. false

24. As the Rodney King incident revealed to the U.S society, most interactions between police and citizens are confrontational in nature.

    a. true
    b. false

25. "Violence prone officers" are often those with personal problems.

    a. true
    b. false

26. Law enforcement officers have disproportionately high rates of divorce and suicide.

    a. true
    b. false

27. Private security officers are outnumbered by police officers at a rate of 3 to 1.

    a. true
    b. false

28. Juveniles have been treated in the same manner by the criminal justice system since 1850; harshly.

    a. true
    b. false

29. In the decisions of <u>Gault</u> and <u>Kent</u>, the Supreme Court established the constitutionality of the principle of <u>parens patriae</u>.

    a. true
    b. false

30. Research and crime statistics clearly indicate that juvenile crime will soon overwhelm the nation.

    a. true
    b. false

31. Girls are more likely to be held for status offenses than boys.

    a. true
    b. false

32. Research indicates that most juveniles who are incarcerated adequate living space and educational opportunities.

    a. true
    b. false

33. The bail system reinforces the basic premise of justice that all people will be treated equally under the law.

    a. true
    b. false

34. Fewer than 10% of all cases ever go to trial.

    a. true
    b. false

35. Many people opt for a plea bargain because they realize they will receive a shorter sentence.

a. true
b. false

36. In some jurisdictions, the use of plea bargains to settle cases may occur in as many as 80% of criminal cases.

a. true
b. false

37. The difference between a jail and a prison is that jails are temporary holding areas and prisons are reserved for longer sentences.

a. true
b. false

38. Research indicates that the poor and the young are more likely to receive prison sentences.

a. true
b. false

39. The majority of states have stricken their death penalty statutes from the books.

a. true
b. false

40. Crime is virtually nonexistant in socialist societies.

a. true
b. false

Multiple Choice

1. The ____________ model of law focuses on crime as a violation of "collective conscious."

a. pluralist
b. functional
c. elite
d. symbolic-interactionist

2. Which theory of law assumes that society consists of many competitive interests struggling for power and control over the legal system?

   a. pluralist
   b. functional
   c. elite
   d. symbolic-interactionist

3. Which perspective does <u>not</u> argue that laws are derived from the shared values and norms of society?

   a. pluralist
   b. functionalist
   c. elite
   d. all of the above believe in consensus

4. Each of the theories for law creation in the text (functional, pluralist, and elite) can be criticized for being:

   a. elitist
   b. class biased
   c. value neutral
   d. one-dimensional

5. The dialectical or crisis model of law creation:

   a. assumes that all laws represent consensus
   b. assumes that laws always reflect the interests of the elite
   c. assumes that the creation of laws is specific to socio-historic circumstances
   d. assumes that what is threatening in one generation is threatening in all generations and thus laws do not change

6. Which of the following is <u>not</u> a central component of criminal law?

   a. the law is legislated by the state in the name of the people
   b. the law is specific in its identification of what is forbidden
   c. the law does not mandate uniform enforcement by the state nor uniform application of the prescribed punishment
   d. the law requires criminal intent to accompany the act

7. The Sherman Anti-Trust Act:

   a. was successful in eliminating corporate monopolization
   b. was implemented to the "full letter of the law"
   c. did not regulate corporate concentration
   d. was used as a strike-breaking tool until the 1930s
   e. both c and d above

8. The Harrison Act of 1914:

a. criminalized the use of drugs
b. was enacted to generate revenue from drug sales
c. was enacted to punish opium addicts
d. medicalized drug addiction
e. both a and b above

9. Research on those convicted of Driving Under the Influence reveals:

a. the majority of people are serving jail time
b. the majority of people are not serving jail time
c. that groups such as MADD have not been influential in effecting changes in legislation
d. lobbying by groups such as MADD have increased the guilt among these individuals

10. Recent research on policing practices indicates that the policing strategy which has existed in the U.S. for most of the 20th century is:

a. professional crime fighting
b. strategic policing
c. problem-solving policing
d. community policing

11. Currently the ___________________ model of policing is seen as a necessity to stop crime.

a. professional crime fighting
b. strategic policing
c. problem-solving policing
d. community policing

12. The "professional crime fighting model" of policing has been criticized for:

a. overlooking hidden crimes
b. creating a separation between the public and the police
c. not dealing with white collar crime
d. all of the above

13. The model of community policing most clearly emerged

a. during the 1880's
b. during the Depression
c. during the 1960's
d. in the early 1990's; after the Los Anglos riots

14. Research indicates that police officers spend approximately ____% of their time on law enforcement.

    a. 100
    b. 75
    c. 50
    d. 20

15. Which of the following factors are important in determining how a police officer will use his/her discretionary judgement in making arrests?

    a. minority status
    b. social class
    c. respect
    d. all of the above
    e. none of the above; decisions are made objectively

16. Officers who are thought to be "violence prone" are:

    a. those with personality disorders
    b. young and improperly trained officers
    c. officers with personal problems
    d. all of the above

17. Police officers:

    a. have high rates of divorce
    b. have high rates of suicide
    c. have many opportunities for corruption
    d. all of the above

18. The movement towards the formation of professional in-groups for police officers has resulted in:

    a. increasing rates of depression among the police
    b. a code of secrecy among the police
    c. seeing "outsiders" as threats
    d. all of the above
    e. both b and c above

19. During the Progressive Period, the guiding principle to govern the treatment of juveniles became:

    a. mala prohibita
    b. mala in se
    c. parens patriae
    d. juvenila characta

20. The Supreme court decisions of Gault and Kent:

    a. reinforced the notion of parens patriae
    b. reinforced the notion of juvenila characta
    c. gave juveniles due process rights
    d. eliminated the death penalty as an option for juveniles

21. Which type of offense are juveniles more likely to commit than older age groups?

    a. violent crimes
    b. white-collar crimes
    c. serious property crimes
    d. all of the above

22. Since the 1970's, juvenile crime has increased most noticeably in the category of:

    a. murder
    b. serious property crime
    c. white-collar crime
    d. none of the above

23. Status offenses:

    a. are committed to improve one's place in society
    b. would not be considered criminal if committed by an adult
    c. would be considered criminal if committed by an adult
    d. include only crimes against property

24. Research on juvenile crime and gang membership indicates:

    a. no relationship between the two
    b. gang membership decreases the likelihood one will engage in violent crime
    c. gang membership increases the likelihood one will engage in violent crime
    d. a decreasing number of poor African-American men are joining gangs because of their fear of incarceration

25. Which of the following is <u>not</u> an example of a status offense?

    a. curfew violations
    b. truancy
    c. incorrigible behavior
    d. larceny

26. A Department of Justice study found that a significant percentage of juveniles who are incarcerated:

    a. are receiving inadequate health care
    b. are receiving inadequate educational opportunities
    c. are receiving inadequate living space
    d. all of the above

27. Less than 10% of cases go to trial because:

    a. there is pressure placed on defendants to plea bargain
    b. there is usually a long time delay between arrest and trial
    c. they are usually thrown out for insufficient evidence
    d. both a and b above

28. Defendants are encouraged to plea bargain for all of the following reasons <u>except:</u>

    a. trial delay
    b. sentencing severity
    c. judge selection
    d. all of the above are tools used by the DA to encourage pleas

29. Studies on sentencing practices reveal that:

    a. the older defendants are more likely to receive prison sentences
    b. race is not related to sentencing
    c. white males are less likely to be sentenced to imprisonment than black males for committing the same offense
    d. sentencing guidelines have been effective in reducing sentence disparity

30. Which of the following factors is thought to have the <u>most</u> significant impact on sentencing?

    a. age
    b. race
    c. class
    d. gender

31. Punishment of an offender should try to achieve which of the following objectives?

    a. rehabilitation
    b. incapacitation
    c. retribution
    d. all of the above

32. Which of the following in <u>not</u> true about probation?

a. clients are easily supervised
b. it is cost-effective
c. it decreases recidivism
d. it removes the offender from the prison environment

33. Which of the following have been suggested as alternatives to incarceration?

a. boot camps
b. intensive probation
c. house arrest
d. all of the above

34. How many states currently have death penalty statutes in effect?

a. 10
b. 22
c. 37
d. 50

35. Who among the following is most likely to support the death penalty?

a. an African-American man
b. an African-American woman
c. a white man
d. a white woman

36. Research on the death penalty indicates that:

a. it effectively serves as a deterrent for violent crime
b. it effectively reduces the overall crime rate
c. abolishing the death penalty increases violent crime
d. none of the above

37. The majority of those incarcerated in the U.S are held

a. in jails
b. in maximum security prisons
c. in comfortable living conditions
d. in new (built after 1950) prisons

38. Which of the following is <u>not</u> a problem currently facing prisoners in the U.S?

    a. over-crowded conditions
    b. AIDS
    c. interpersonal violence
    d. all of the above are problems facing prisoners

39. Advocates of probation argue all of the following <u>except</u>:

    a. it is a cost effective alternative to incarceration
    b. encourages rehabilitation
    c. it reduces recidivism
    d. it enables probation officers to easily supervise their charges

40. Research on crime in developing nations indicates that crime:

    a. does not change with the modernization process
    b. is no different than crime in the industrialized nations
    c. often reflects economic situations
    d. centers mostly on violent crimes

<u>Fill in the Blanks</u>

1. The ____________________ perspective of law creation stresses the importance of understanding law in relation to the socio-historic circumstances in which it evolves.

2. A _________ is defined as an act for which a society provides formally sanctioned punishment.

3. The _______________________________ model of policing relies on a disciplined, quasi-military police force to insure social order.

4. The term _________________ refers to the court acting in place of the child's parents to provide for the needs of the child.

5. The most cost-effective method for sanctioning offenders is ____ ___________.

Matching

1. functional model of law.
2. mala in se acts
3. this theory argues that laws reflect the interests of a few, powerful individuals
4. due to the way this law was enforced, it basically criminalized drug use
5. this act was the first major effort of the government to control commerce
6. he studied the Syracuse police department
7. the style of policing which stresses sting operations
8. 37 states have this
9. the type of crime juveniles are most likely to commit
10. examples of status offenses
11. crimes in which the participants do not see themselves victimized by the illicit transaction
12. the type of crime prevalent in third world nations
13. an act which is considered criminal if committed by minors, but not by adults
14. this model of policing involves developing a working relationship between police and the community
15. this model of policing involves controlling crime and crime-solving
16. the requirement that the accused post a specific amount of money to theoretically guarantee he/she will not flee
17. an alternative to bail, when the person is seen as a good risk
18. when the accused agrees to plead guilty in exchange for a lesser charge or sentence
19. the chief alternative to prison
20. actions which are wrong because they are inherently evil

A. Crime Index Offenses
B. serious property crime
C. Sherman Anti-Trust Act
D. James Q. Wilson
E. elite perspective
F. Emile Durkheim
G. political crime
H. probation
I. victimless crimes
J. strategic policing
K. truancy and curfew violations
L. the death penalty
M. community policing
N. bail
O. status offense
P. Harrison Act
Q. mala in se
R. professional crime fighting
S. plea bargain
T. release on recognizance

ANSWERS TO CHAPTER 11

True/False

1.	True	21.	True
2.	False	22.	True
3.	False	23.	False
4.	False	24.	False
5.	True	25.	True
6.	True	26.	True
7.	True	27.	False
8.	True	28.	False
9.	False	29.	False
10.	True	30.	False
11.	True	31.	True
12.	False	32.	False
13.	False	33.	False
14.	True	34.	True
15.	True	35.	True
16.	False	36.	True
17.	False	37.	False
18.	True	38.	True
19.	True	39.	False
20.	False	40.	False

Multiple Choice

1.	b	21.	c
2.	a	22.	a
3.	c	23.	b
4.	d	24.	c
5.	c	25.	d
6.	c	26.	d
7.	e	27.	d
8.	e	28.	d
9.	d	29.	c
10.	a	30.	b
11.	d	31.	a
12.	d	32.	a
13.	c	33.	d
14.	d	34.	c
15.	d	35.	c
16.	d	36.	d
17.	d	37.	b
18.	e	38.	d
19.	c	39.	d
20.	c	40.	c

Fill in the Blanks

1. Dialectical or Crisis
2. Crime
3. professional crime-fighting
4. Parens Patriae
5. Probation

Matching

1. F
2. C
3. E
4. P
5. A
6. D
7. J
8. L
9. B
10. K
11. I
12. G
13. O
14. M
15. R
16. N
17. T
18. S
19. H
20. Q

9. The repeated planting of a single crop results in the depletion of minerals in the soil.

   a. true
   b. false

10. Natural droughts are important ecologically for decreasing the amount of topsoil which is washed away.

   a. true
   b. false

11. The clearing of rain forests is important in gaining rich topsoil.

   a. true
   b. false

12. Currently 80% of the population of developing countries depend on wood for cooking and heating.

   a. true
   b. false

13. Total recovery of biomass levels may take up to 1000 years in some areas where the land has been severely abused.

   a. true
   b. false

14. Desertification is a process that results in expanding desserts by tree removal.

   a. true
   b. false

15. The ecological relationship between rainfall, forests and soil is <u>not</u> an interdependent one.

   a. true
   b. false

16. According to the IUCN, over the next 20 years, one-fifth of all plant and animal species may disappear.

   a. true
   b. false

17. It is estimated that as many as 1000 animals are in danger of extinction.

   a. true
   b. false

18. Increased technology and the failure to regulate the use of these advances are primarily responsible for recent environmental damage.

    a. true
    b. false

19. The population of the U.S. currently generates over 1.5 trillion pounds of trash annually.

    a. true
    b. false

20. During five days in 1952, 4000 Londoners were killed by air pollution and smog.

    a. true
    b. false

21. Acidity levels in water supplies has been known to turn blond hair temporarily green.

    a. true
    b. false

22. Acid rain has had devastating effects on physical structures such as the Statue of Liberty and Independence Hall.

    a. true
    b. false

23. The rate of depletion of the ozone layer has been slowed during the past decade.

    a. true
    b. false

24. If there were a halt to emissions of chemicals into the atmosphere right now, damage could still continue for possibly as long as 125 years.

    a. true
    b. false

25. The greenhouse effect is caused primarily by the natural warming of the earth through sunlight.

    a. true
    b. false

26. Many scientists believe that the influence of the greenhouse effect is unavoidable.

    a. true
    b. false

27. Fortunately, government regulation of the burning of fossil fuels has had an important effect in most U.S. cities.

    a. true
    b. false

28. Since World War II, most Americans have developed a "throwaway" mentality.

    a. true
    b. false

29. Since World War II, the amount of toxic waste produced in the U.S. has increased to a dangerous level.

    a. true
    b. false

30. It is generally accepted that over 90% of hazardous waste is disposed of properly

    a. true
    b. false

31. The EPA's estimation that almost 2,000 disposal sites in the U.S. are in desperate need of clean-up, is thought to be a greatly inflated.

    a. true
    b. false

32. Union Carbide has enjoyed one of the best safety records among major industrial corporations.

    a. true
    b. false

33. The pollution of coastal water in the Mediterranean Sea is mainly the result of the direct pumping of sewage by coastal cities into the sea.

    a. true
    b. false

34. Over 90% of energy in the U.S. is derived from non-renewable sources.

a. true
b. false

35. The Industrial nations consume almost twice as much energy as developing countries.

a. true
b. false

36. The U.S. has always imported a significant percentage of energy.

a. true
b. false

37. The development of hydropower as a renewable energy source has occurred almost exclusively in the U.S.

a. true
b. false

38. The accidental release of radioactivity can only occur during certain stages of the production of nuclear energy.

a. true
b. false

39. Between 1980 and 1988, funding for energy research and development significantly declined in the U.S.

a. true
b. false

40. Nuclear power is not an adequate source of alternative energy technology because it is dangerous and costly.

a. true
b. false

Multiple Choice

1. Which of the following is not a book which has been instrumental in sparking public awareness concerning the environment?

a. The Population Bomb
b. The Ecological Wasteland
c. The Silent Spring
d. all of the above

2. The deterioration of the environment has taken place primarily:

   a. during the past generation
   b. during the past 20 years
   c. during the past 200 years
   d. during the past 1000 years

3. Industrialization had serious implications for the environment because of:

   a. population growth that has accompanied medical advances
   b. technological advances which harmed the environment
   c. industrial expansion which threatened the environment's natural resources
   d. all of the above

4. The science which deals with the interrelationships between living things and their environment is:

   a. sociology
   b. ecology
   c. environmentalism
   d. physiology

5. The balance of the ecosystem is significantly affected by:

   a. the possible extinction of any animal
   b. the ice age
   c. humans
   d. natural disasters
   e. all of the above

6. Which of the following is <u>not</u> a way in which humans have affected the environment?

   a. the natural growth of the human species
   b. the human appetite for natural materials
   c. the consistent replacement of natural materials which are depleted
   d. rapid technological development

7. A ______________ resource is inexhaustible and will always exist regardless of human usage.

   a. renewable
   b. non-renewable
   c. flow
   d. perpetual

8. Fossil fuel is a prime example of which type of resource?

a. renewable
b. non-renewable
c. flow
d. perpetual

9. The acid rain dilemma is a result of:

a. industrial pollution
b. auto pollution
c. improper management of wood resources during the middle ages
d. both a and b

10. A federal survey found that U.S. farmlands:

a. were losing topsoil at an "excessive rate"
b. were not losing topsoil at a dangerous level
c. have enjoyed an increase in productive capability
d. have not been affected by soil erosion

11. The erosion of topsoil leads to:

a. decreased crop production
b. the use of chemicals to enhance soil conditions
c. deforestation
d. all of the above

12. The problem of deforestation appears to be most serious in:

a. industrialized nations
b. developing nations
c. Europe
d. none of the above

13. Deforestation is particularly problematic in developing nations because:

a. the use of wood in cooking and heating is much lower than in the industrial nations
b. they are less likely to replant than industrialized nations
c. they are more likely to use methods such as "slash and burn" which is harsher on the land than bulldozing
d. all of the above

14. Desertification is closely related to:

a. atrification
b. mega-extinction
c. deforestation
d. pollution

15. The Institutional Union for Conservation of Nature and Natural Resources (IUCN) estimates that:

    a. 25,000 plants are threatened with extinction
    b. 25,000 animals are threatened with extinction
    c. 1,000 plants are threatened with extinction
    d. plants and animals are not in danger of extinction in significant numbers

16. The most threatened category of life currently is:

    a. amphibians
    b. mammals
    c. birds
    d. insects

17. Preservation of endangered species can best be helped through:

    a. protection of natural wetlands
    b. protection of natural forests
    c. protection of watery areas
    d. all of the above

18. Humankind's transformation of the earth's environment began:

    a. during pre-historic time
    b. with the introduction of agriculture
    c. with colonialism
    d. with industrialization

19. Increases in technology:

    a. constitute one of the most significant factors in the deterioration of the environment
    b. have allowed for regulatory measures for the environment
    c. have occurred with equal increased in environmental awareness
    d. are not important when considering environmental issues

20. The condition known as a "real pea-souper" refers to:

    a. a pollutant that has effected the U.S. since 1953
    b. an Englishman who really likes his soup
    c. an environmental measure taken to reduce smog
    d. green-yellow smog of London

21. A result of the 1952 London air pollution disaster was:

    a. increased environmental awareness in London
    b. the declaration of many cities in the United Kingdom as "smoke free zones"
    c. the elimination of London smog by the early 1960's
    d. all of the above

22. The major source of nitrogen oxide pollution in the U.S. is:

a. power plants in the Southeast
b. power plants in the Midwest
c. automobiles
d. electrical utilities

23. One of the most serious effects of acid rain on the environment is:

a. the aquatic life in tens of thousands of lakes has been destroyed
b. lakes and rivers in North America have dried up
c. the organic matter in acified lakes has doubled
d. fish have grown to previously unseen dimensions

24. Effects of acid rain on humankind include all of the following <u>except:</u>

a. drinking water is contaminated with heavy metals
b. diarrhea in young children
c. blond hair can be turned temporarily green
d. contaminated water has increased the size of newborns

25. Which of the following has <u>not</u> been affected by acid rain?

a. the forests of West Germany
b. the Sichuan province in China
c. the Washington Monument
d. all of the above have been affected
e. only a and b above have been affected

26. Research indicates that the hole in the ozone over the Antarctic:

a. is smaller than the size of a nickel
b. is larger than the state of New Jersey
c. is larger than twice the size of the continental U.S.
d. is a figment of some scientists' imagination

27. A direct effect of the depletion of the ozone layer is a rise in the rates of:

a. skin cancer
b. eye diseases
c. threats to plants
d. all of the above

28. A direct consequence of the "greenhouse effect" includes:

    a. a decrease in average global temperatures
    b. a reduction in the size of lakes
    c. the oceans of the world will decrease
    d. the Midwestern U.S. will increase its farm production

29. Waste collection and disposal:

    a. is a $20 billion a year business
    b. is conducted by the EPA
    c. has worked efficiently and safely
    d. has dwindled in popularity and need

30. The problem of toxic waste has:

    a. decreased due to the "throwaway mentality"
    b. increased due to the large scale production of wood, cotton and wool in the U.S.
    c. decreased in the past decade
    d. increased due to the sheer number of materials which produce toxic waste

31. According to the U.S. Office of Technology Assessment, the state with the highest number of hazardous waste sites is:

    a. California
    b. New York
    c. New Jersey
    d. Michigan

32. Which of the following is <u>not</u> a consequence of the dumping of hazardous wastes?

    a. contamination of water supplies
    b. human infertility
    c. contamination of local water supplies only
    d. cancer

33. The pollution of coastal waters:

    a. is primarily a problem limited to the U.S.
    b. has not yet been addressed by the United Nations
    c. has not been fully eliminated in the U.S. by the Clean Water Act
    d. is always unintended

34. The world's commercial energy is consumed mostly by:

a. industrial production
b. housing
c. transportation
d. health

35. The country which is the largest consumer of energy is:

a. South Africa
b. United States
c. China
d. Japan

36. Which of the following activities would have a serious impact on reducing energy consumption?

a. the use of more efficient light bulbs and fixtures
b. the use of more American-made cars
c. adoption of the conservation policies of Third World countries
d. all of the above

37. Almost 1/4 of the energy that is used internationally:

a. comes form renewable sources
b. comes from nuclear power sources
c. is consumed by Third World countries
d. is hydroelectric power

38. The largest renewable energy source is:

a. hydropower
b. coal
c. wood
d. solar energy

39. High-level waste from spent reactor fuel:

a. should be reprocessed and stored at a high-level site
b. can be reused by military personnel for experimental weaponry
c. does not pose a significant danger to the environment
d. should be encapsuled in metal containers and buried

40. Environmental protection during the 1980's was problematic due to:

a. budget cuts
b. deregulation
c. a focus on nuclear power
d. all of the above

Fill in the Blanks

1. The environmental system in which the interrelationship between living things and the environment takes place is the __________.

2. The term ______________ applies to the point at which there is total restoration of living plant matter on forested areas.

3. The gradual warming of the earth is known as the _____________.

4. The EPA has been funded by legislation called the ____________ to cleanup those disposal sites which are on the "national priority list".

5. ____________________ consumes over 1/4 of the world's energy and is considered to be the most wasteful user of energy.

Matching

1. The worst administration for dealing with environmental issues
2. Has a strong commitment to dealing with environmental issues
3. he was one of the first to define the new science "ecology"
4. this resource is inexhaustible
5. this resource exists in finite amounts and cannot be renewed
6. another word for renewable resources
7. the clearing of wooded areas
8. green-yellow smog of London
9. when sulfuric acid and nitrogen oxide are produced and combined with water
10. the U.S dependency on convenience rather than durability in their consumerism
11. this state has the highest rate of hazardous waste dumps
12. this state housed the Union Carbide toxic tragedy
13. the most common renewable fuel
14. Chernobyl
15. this state obtains close to half of its electrical energy from renewable sources
16. Three Mile Island
17. the melting of fuel rods which releases radioactive steam into the atmosphere
18. radioactive elements
19. gradual warming of the earth
20. the cheapest and cleanest source of electricity

A. perpetual
B. "real pea-souper"
C. Rachel Carson
D. throwaway mentality
E. New Jersey
F. Reagan administration

G. wood
H. non-renewable
I. nuclear disaster in the U.S.
J. West Virginia
K. isotopes
L. acid rain
M. hydropower
N. California
O. meltdown
P. Clinton administration
Q. deforestation
R. nuclear disaster
S. greenhouse effect
T. flow

ANSWERS TO CHAPTER 12

True/False

1. True
2. False
3. False
4. False
5. True
6. False
7. False
8. True
9. True
10. False
11. False
12. True
13. True
14. True
15. False
16. True
17. True
18. True
19. False
20. True
21. True
22. True
23. False
24. True
25. False
26. True
27. False
28. True
29. True
30. False
31. False
32. False
33. True
34. True
35. True
36. False
37. False
38. False
39. True
40. True

Multiple Choice

1. b
2. c
3. d
4. b
5. e
6. c
7. d
8. b
21. d
22. c
23. a
24. d
25. d
26. c
27. d
28. b

9.	d	29.	a
10.	a	30.	d
11.	d	31.	c
12.	b	32.	c
13.	b	33.	c
14.	c	34.	a
15.	a	35.	b
16.	d	36.	a
17.	d	37.	a
18.	b	38.	e
19.	a	39.	a
20.	d	40.	d

Fill in the Blanks

1. Ecosystem,
2. Total biomass
3. Greenhouse effect
4. Superfund
5. The United States

Matching

1. C
2. F
3. P
4. A
5. H
6. T
7. Q
8. B
9. L
10. D
11. E
12. J
13. G
14. R
15. N
16. I
17. O
18. K
19. S
20. M

CHAPTER 13

Population growth is an important factor in the destruction of the natural ecosystem. This chapter examines population growth worldwide and the impact of efforts to control this growth. Also, the problems of urbanization, housing, and homelessness are examined in detail.

A. THE POPULATION CRISIS

Other issues in the world arena besides environmental concerns deserve attention. Since World War II, the world's population has grown at an unprecedented rate, particularly in the poorer, developing nations. Cultural values and economic necessity make large families desirable for many poor in other nations. Over-population has serious implications.

1. Rapid population growth is a relatively recent phenomenon. Three phases of population growth are identified with the most extensive growth occurring during the second or "transitional growth stage." While industrialized nations now experience minimal population growth, falling mortality rates and continued high birth rates cause exorbitant population growth in developing or underdeveloped nations.
    a. This trend will cause a maldistribution of the world's population. Hunger on a massive scale will result.
    b. Rapid urbanization in the Third World presents serious problems. Inadequate facilities to house the amount of population in need of shelter often results in the creation of shantytowns, slums or squatter settlements.

These areas lack sanitation, which causes serious health problems. These cities also do not have employment to offer their citizens. Food shortages and inadequate diets are the norm.

c. The extent of the problem of rapid population growth in the Third World requires action. Population control policies may be the only effective means of curbing growth. The success of China's one-child family policy is reviewed. Some policies practiced in other areas are discussed.

B. PROBLEMS OF THE URBAN ENVIRONMENT

With the rise of the modern metropolis, cities came to be portrayed as characterized by isolation. Many in the U.S. hold negative perceptions of cities with their vast array of social problems.

1. The deterioration of our nation's cities is the end result of years of governmental neglect and exploitation by property owners. Property re-evaluation may drive poor residents out of their homes.
2. Upper and middle class flight has caused a fiscal crisis in the cities. Despite an eroded tax base, cities are still expected to maintain necessary services. At the same time, federal funds available to cities have been declining, further compounding the problem.

C. THE GROWING HOUSING CRISIS IN THE U.S.

Although the increased standard of living found many in the U.S.

with a higher level of housing, this did not occur for the poor or rural inhabitants. The increasing cost of housing currently puts benefits such as owning a home, out of the reach of even middle class Americans.

1. Not only can people not afford new homes but increasingly they cannot afford the expenses necessary to keep the homes they have. Rents have also risen steadily due in part to governmental withdrawal from low rent housing and the private sector's unwillingness to continue rental housing for low and middle income families. Thus, an increasing proportion of these families' income is spent on housing.
2. The problem of homelessness is presented here. The difficulties in assessing the number of homeless are discussed.
    a. Although myths and stereotypes about the homeless are commonly held, research demonstrates that this is a diverse population. Currently the fastest growing segment of the U.S. homeless population is families with children.
        b. Some efforts to deal with the problem of the homeless are presented.

SELF-TEST

True/False

1. The Malthusian theory was proposed in the late 1700s.

   a. true
   b. false

2. The world's population is increasing by one million people every four or five days.

   a. true
   b. false

3. Industrialized nations tend to have higher growth rates than developing countries.

   a. true
   b. false

4. In many Third World countries, children are seen as investments both economically and emotionally to their parents.

   a. true
   b. false

5. It is believed that high fertility rates contribute to women's dominant position in developing countries.

   a. true
   b. false

6. Population growth is highest during the initial stage of development.

   a. true
   b. false

7. Most Industrialized nations have had low population growth since World War II.

   a. true
   b. false

8. 40% of those in developing countries are between the ages of 15 and 40, the childbearing years.

   a. true

b. false

9. It is estimated that 95% of the next billion people will be born into the poorest nations of the world's community.

a. true
b. false

10. Rapid urbanization is currently only a problem in developing countries.

a. true
b. false

11. In some Third World cities, squatters may make up the majority of the population.

a. true
b. false

12. In developing nations, as much as 90% of the population is sometimes unemployed.

a. true
b. false

13. In 1950, China lowered the legislated minimum age of marriage to encourage younger marriages.

a. true
b. false

14. The goal of China is to have a population which does not exceed 1.2 billion by the year 2000.

a. true
b. false

15. Most developing nations have followed China's model of controlling population growth through legal provisions.

a. true
b. false

16. Extended breastfeeding significantly lowers the probability of pregnancy.

a. true
b. false

17. Women in developing countries are more likely to have abortions than those in industrialized nations.

    a. true
    b. false

18. Soap operas have been used by the government in Mexico City to convince women to practice contraception.

    a. true
    b. false

19. In Thailand, vasectomy festivals have been a successful method of controlling births.

    a. true
    b. false

20. Simmel's and Wirth's view of city life were assessed by your authors as accurate.

    a. true
    b. false

21. The poor are primarily responsible for the deterioration of U.S. cities.

    a. true
    b. false

22. The first government program to "renew" the city occurred in 1965.

    a. true
    b. false

23. The Federal Housing Administration (FHA) had considerable success in urban renewal programs in the 1950's and 1960's.

    a. true
    b. false

24. The Model Cities Program, considered to be the most comprehensive attempt to meet the needs of the poor, fell far short of its objectives.

    a. true
    b. false

13. Research on children worldwide indicates:

    a. that less than 1/3 of children under 10 suffer from malnutrition
    b. that half the children under 6 suffer from malnutrition
    c. that malnutrition is a social problem which has been effectively eliminated
    d. that malnutrition is only a problem in a few developing countries

14. Food shortages in the Third World have the following effect:

    a. anemia
    b. blindness
    c. reduced weight and height
    d. all of the above

15. To slow population growth, China:

    a. made available a variety of birth control options
    b. passed legislation to encourage teenage marriages
    c. withheld food supplies to peasants
    d. put forth a propaganda campaign based on traditional cultural values

16. Some Third World nations are experiencing declines in overall fertility as a result of all of the following <u>except:</u>

    a. extended periods of breastfeeding
    b. educational programs on contraception
    c. decreased usage of female sterilization
    d. all of the above

17. Birth control in industrial countries:

    a. most often take the form of oral contraceptives along with abortion
    b. is usually discouraged by educational programs
    c. typically involves legal measures from the government
    d. is based on the universal practice of celibacy

18. Which of the following is true regarding the use of contraception?

    a. women are most likely to use what is made available by the local government
    b. women are most likely to use what is emphasized by the local government
    c. women are not likely to use contraception under any circumstances
    d. both a and b

19. Which of the following cities has <u>not</u> lost population recently?

    a. New York city
    b. London
    c. Philadelphia
    d. Mexico city

20. Internationally, major cities like New York, Chicago, London, Paris and Moscow:

    a. are projected to double in population by the year 2000
    b. are projected to have their population cut in half by the year 2000
    c. have been losing population in the past decade
    d. have been gaining population recently

21. Which of the following sociologists did <u>not</u> have a negative view of the city and urban life?

    a. Georg Simmel
    b. Louis Worth
    c. Herbert Gans
    d. all of the above were critical of city life

22. He believed that those who lived in the city were subjected to "nervous stimulation".

    a. Georg Simmel
    b. Karl Marx
    c. Herbert Gans
    d. Louis Wirth

23. __________________ argued that urban life led to a loosening of traditional social bonds and caused isolation among its residents.

    a. Karl Marx
    b. Louis Wirth
    c. Thomas Malthus
    d. Georg Simmel

24. The deterioration of the city:

    a. was brought about by years of neglect and exploitation
    b. was caused primarily by actions of the poor
    c. has occurred over a short period of time
    d. has yet to occur on any great scale

25. The Federal Housing Administration was established:

a. to meet the growing needs of the homeless
b. to meet the needs of women and children in poverty
c. to help people secure adequate housing
d. to create descent housing in Third World countries

26. The Model Cities Programs, and other programs which are similar, often fail because:

a. the poor do not know how to take care of their homes
b. they focus too much on health care and education in these communities and not enough on housing
c. they minimize community participation in the decision making process
d. all of the above

27. The shift in administrative policy from the construction of public housing to "public assistance" occurred mainly because:

a. public assistance would better meet the needs of the poor
b. there was no urban space available for constructing public housing
c. public housing was twice as expensive as rent subsidies for low-income residents in existing dwellings
d. all of the above

28. Clinton's "Empowerment Zone"

a. provides funding to every major city in the U.S
b. provides intensive funding to a limited number of areas
c. has already been deemed a failure in public opinion polls
d. none of the above

29. A major factor causing the loss of property in urban areas is:

a. destruction so that public housing can be created
b. natural disasters
c. reassessments
d. none of the above

30. The erosion of the tax base is caused primarily by:

a. suburbanization
b. gentrification
c. nationalization
d. sterilization

31. Which of the following is <u>not</u> an effect of suburbanization?

a. the erosion of the tax base
b. segregation of minorities in the cities
c. segregation of affluent whites in the suburbs
d. increased financial stability of large cities

32. In 1993, the average price of an existing single-family home was:

a. $45,000
b. $90,000
c. $107,000
d. $250,000

33. The decline in home ownership has most drastically affected:

a. retired senior citizens
b. families with children
c. young households without children
d. property owners interested in renting

34. The Federal Government's involvement in housing assistance:

a. declined significantly in the 1980s
b. increased dramatically in the 1980s
c. has remained consistently low in the last 20 years
d. has remained consistently high in the past 20 years

35. The study conducted by the Federal Reserve Board indicates that:

a. poor people receive more loans than the affluent
b. whites receive more loans than minorities
c. whites receive fewer loans than minorities
d. all of the above

36. Which of the following is <u>not</u> an explanation for the scarcity of low-income housing in the U.S?

a. federal budget cuts
b. inflation
c. rent-regulated apartments being held off the markets by greedy landlords
d. the increasing burden of rent
e. all of the above

37. Since the 1987 hearings of the Select Committee on Children, Youth and Families:

    a. the situation of the homeless has improved ten-fold
    b. the number of people who are homeless has decreased
    c. the number of people who are homeless has increased
    d. homelessness has not been an important issue on the U.S agenda

38. It is estimated that approximately __________ U.S. citizens are homeless.

    a. 10,000
    b. 1 million
    c. 3 million
    d. 10 million

39. Recent studies of homelessness show that:

    a. the majority have a high school education
    b. the majority have a college degree
    c. the majority are generally uneducated
    d. the majority are clinically insane

40. The fastest growing segment of the displaced population in the U.S. is:

    a. young minority men
    b. young white men
    c. families with children
    d. children

Fill in the Blanks

1. A home made of wood, paper, tin or other available materials is known as a ________________.

2. In 1979 China instituted its ____________________ policy to stem population growth.

3. The ______________________ was instituted as part of the War on Poverty and has been perceived by most as a failure.

4. The renewal of old neighborhoods by affluent professionals is __ ________________.

5. The most rapidly growing segment of the homeless population of the U.S. is _________.

Matching

1. Thomas Malthus
2. theory of demographic transition
3. the stage at which there is both a high birth and high death rate
4. the stage at which the death rate declines and the birth rate is maintained
5. the stage at which birth and death rates are low, and growth is minimal
6. China
7. the most common form of contraception in developing countries
8. the most common form of contraception in industrialized countries
9. vasectomy festivals are held here
10. couples are given a free trip to Mecca for practicing birth control in this country
11. he thought that city life caused "nervous stimulation"
12. he did not see city life as negative
13. this agency was established to help people secure housing
14. Model Cities Program
15. provision of housing for low-income populations through private concerns who are given tax benefits and below-market financing
16. the exodus of more affluent groups from the city
17. Select Committee on Children, Youth and Families
18. the number of homeless people in the U.S
19. exodus of affluent populations decreases revenues of cities
20. the renewal of old neighborhoods by affluent populations

A. initial stage
B. Indonesia
C. believed that populations grow geometrically
D. Georg Simmel
E. War on Poverty
F. this provides a model for understanding population growth
G. one child family
H. erosion of the tax base
I. female sterilization
J. incipient decline stage
K. dealt with the issue of homelessness
L. Thailand
M. FHA
N. Herbert Gans
O. 3 million
P. assisted housing
Q. condoms
R. gentrification
S. suburbanization
T. transitional growth stage

ANSWERS TO CHAPTER 13

True/False

1.	True	21.	False
2.	True	22.	False
3.	False	23.	False
4.	True	24.	True
5.	False	25.	True
6.	False	26.	True
7.	False	27.	True
8.	True	28.	False
9.	True	29.	False
10.	False	30.	False
11.	True	31.	False
12.	True	32.	True
13.	False	33.	True
14.	True	34.	False
15.	False	35.	True
16.	True	36.	True
17.	False	37.	True
18.	True	38.	False
19.	True	39	True
20.	True.	40.	False

Multiple Choice

1.	b	21.	c
2.	d	22.	a
3.	a	23.	b
4.	c	24.	a
5.	d	25.	c
6.	b	26.	c
7.	d	27.	c
8.	d	28.	b
9.	d	29.	c
10.	d	30.	a
11.	d	31.	d
12.	d	32.	c
13.	b	33.	b
14.	d	34.	a
15.	a	35.	b
16.	c	36.	e
17.	a	37.	c
18.	d	38.	c
19.	d	39.	a
20.	c	40.	c

Fill in the Blanks

1. Shantytown
2. One child policy
3. Model Cities Program
4. Gentrification
5. Families

Matching

1. C
2. F
3. A
4. T
5. J
6. G
7. I
8. Q
9. L
10. B
11. D
12. N
13. M
14. E
15. P
16. S
17. K
18. O
19. H
20. R

CHAPTER 14

This final chapter reemphasizes the inequality present in the U.S. society and calls for social change.

A. TAKING A STAND ON SOCIAL PROBLEMS

The final section of the book encourages readers to initiate change in order to alter institutions and policies that are inadequate.

1. When individuals recognize that others experience similar problems and recognize that the social system is the origin of these problems, <u>social movements</u> develop.
2. Although social movements vary in size and objectives, they all strive to influence society. This text ends by issuing a challenge to readers to become involved in movements for social change.

SELF-TEST

True/False

1. The U.S. is a society in which all people are treated equally, regardless of race, gender or class.

    a. true
    b. false

2. The conflict perspective places emphasis on social change.

    a. true
    b. false

3. In the U.S. it has been popularly believed that social problems are the result of individual failure.

    a. true
    b. false

4. Historically politicians have been immune from internal and external pressure.

    a. true
    b. false

5. According to a 1991 survey of college students, over 60% felt that it is very important to help others who are in need.

    a. true
    b. false

Multiple Choice

1. This text has used the:

    a. functional perspective
    b. conflict perspective
    c. symbolic-interactionist perspective
    d. all of the above

2. Social change is most likely to be initiated by:

    a. those in power
    b. women
    c. men
    d. those who perceive that their interests are not being met

3. Which conditions must exist for a social movement to develop?

   a. inequality
   b. individuals must recognize their problems are shared by others
   c. individuals must see the social system as the source of a problem
   d. all of the above

4. Which of the following organizations is associated with the human rights movement?

   a. Greenpeace
   b. Amnesty International
   c. Democrats United
   d. Parents United

5. Students have been involved in which of the following social movements?

   a. civil rights movement
   b. anti-war movement during the Vietnam War
   c. human rights
   d. all of the above

Fill in the Blanks

1. A ________________ is an issue-oriented group that organizes to take a stand for or against a specific social issue and works to get that position written into public policy.

ANSWERS TO CHAPTER 14

True/False

1. False
2. True
3. True
4. False
5. True

Multiple Choice

1. b
2. d
3. d
4. b
5. d

Fill in the Blank

1. Social Movement